P9-DMP-123

Publisher's Note

DOCTOR TOM DOOLEY, MY STORY is an abridgement, especially prepared for young readers, of *Deliver Us From Evil, The Edge of Tomorrow,* and *The Night They Burned The Mountain.*

Doctor Tom Dooley, My Story

by

THOMAS A. DOOLEY, M.D.

Ariel Books · New York

Copyright © 1956, 1958, 1960 by Thomas A. Dooley

Library of Congress catalog card number 60-9734

Third printing February, 1961

Published simultaneously in Canada by Ambassador Books, Ltd.

MANUFACTURED IN THE UNITED STATES OF AMERICA

Contents

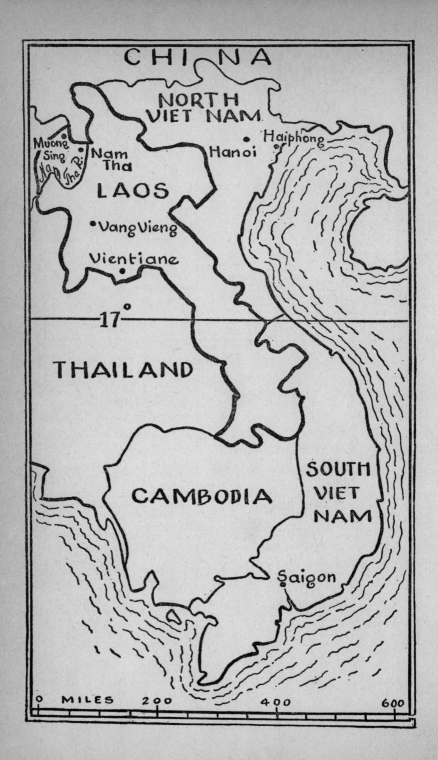

I Get My Orders

Captain Amberson tossed a sheaf of notes and sketches at me. "Dooley, your job will be to help build refugee camps. Look at these—they'll give you the general idea."

Dr. Julius Amberson was head of the Preventive Medicine Unit in Haiphong; I was a Naval Medical Officer, J.G. attached to his unit. This was the year 1954. The French defeat at Dien Bien Phu had passed into history and that Red victory had been nailed down at Geneva in a peace treaty that split Viet Nam in half: the north for the Communists, the south for the non-Communists. According to the terms of the treaty any non-Communist caught in the north was entitled to migrate to the south if that was his wish. The surprise was that hundreds of thousands of people were willing to give up everything they held dear, their country, their homes, their friends and their livelihood for the simple privilege of living in freedom. On their way to the Free World, most of these despairing refugees had to pass through Haiphong. Our directive read that we were "to provide humanitarian and medical attention." That meant refugee camps.

1

"Get going and don't bother me about details," Captain Amberson concluded.

Dr. Amberson was one of the reasons why I had chosen the Navy for my career. He was a great leader. He knew how to delegate authority. You don't talk back to that type of man. "Aye, aye, sir," I said. But I could not conceal from myself the fact that at the moment I didn't know the difference between a refugee camp and a playground for girls.

That night I couldn't sleep. I lay sweating on my bed in that hot, smelly, dying city of Haiphong trying not to be afraid. In college and medical school I had taken courses in everything from Aristotle to Zoology. But unfortunately a course in refugee-camp-building had not been included in my education.

I was billetted in the Continental, one of Haiphong's two hotels. We did not have American-type plumbing or running water. We did have the largest cockroaches and rats I have ever seen. When you stepped toward those cockroaches, instead of running away they ran to you. The rats were large enough to saddle and they loved to fight.

There was a small dance hall in the first of the Continental's two floors. I had been in Haiphong only a few days, but already I knew every song in the repertoire. I could tell the time just by listening. When "Blues In The Night" started, it was 9:30. At 10:00 it was "Tea For Two." At 11:30 "Don't Stay Away Too Long." The shop always closed with a stirring performance of the Marseillaise.

Now they were playing "Don't Stay Away Too Long." It was 11:30. A mosquito had stowed away inside my net and was contributing its two cents' worth of whine to the official music. I slapped at the thing but it got away. I asked myself a question that has haunted so many other young Americans caught in far away places: "What am *I* doing here?"

In a sense I was on this mission behind the Bamboo Curtain because I had asked for it. I had volunteered for the job. I could have quit, I could have gone back aboard a nice, clean ship. I might even have gone home. . . . That night in my discouraged mood I cursed myself for a fool.

For as long as I could remember, I had wanted to be a doctor. Now, at 27, I was an M.D., although a very green one. Anyway, I consoled myself, you are one young doctor who is *not* going to lack patients. From what I had already seen of Haiphong, I was going to crowd more practice in malaria, yaws, beriberi, smallpox, leprosy and cholera into a few months than most doctors see in a lifetime. And even though I was only a fledgling surgeon, I knew that I was going to be called on to do operations that text-books never mention. I thought of the atrocity stories I had heard. What do you do for children who have had chopsticks driven into their inner ears? What do you do for old women whose collarbones have been shattered by rifle butts? How do you treat an old priest who has had nails driven into his skull to make a mockery of the Crown of Thorns?

But at the moment what was worrying me most was that refugee camp. Never before had I been forced to accept real responsibility. Now I had been told to help build a tent city big enough to hold a shifting population of between 10,000 and 15,000 people. And on my own, I had sworn to myself that if I did nothing else, I was going to teach at least some of those refugees to understand and trust Americans. Communist propaganda had made those refugees fear and distrust everything that was made in America. I would have to talk to those men, women and children across a barrier of suspicion and terror. It wasn't going to be an easy job.

No wonder I couldn't sleep; no wonder I tossed back and forth until dawn on my sweaty bed. Then, suddenly, I thought of Albert Schweitzer. Ever since I first went to medical school his work had been one of the great inspirations of my life. A world-famous organist, Dr. Schweitzer had left a brilliant concert career and an easy life to study medicine so that he could go to Africa and found a jungle hospital where the poorest of the poor could be cured of their ills.

Albert Schweitzer believes that men of medicine have a special mission: they must go forth amongst the "have-nots" in far-off lands and do what has to be done, in the name of God and Man.

Instinctively I began to say the *Our Father* as I had every day since I was a child: "And deliver us from evil." At that moment I sensed, however dimly, the purpose behind my being in Indo-China.

I put the flashlight back in its place under my pillow, tucked the mosquito net in tightly—and went to sleep.

CHAPTER TWO

Camp de la Pagode

Situated at the mouth of the delta on the Gulf of Tonkin, only about a hundred miles from the southern frontier of the Chinese province of Kwangsi, Haiphong rates as the best port south of Hong Kong. But even in its best days it was a city of slums, muck and squalor, a rat-infested city that had grown used to the flies and mosquitoes that swarmed through it.

In normal times the population of Haiphong was about 100,000 but in August, 1954, it had been at least doubled by the grey tides of refugees that swept into the city. With baskets and bundles, they sprawled in the streets, gutters and alleys around the bazaar and covered the parks like so many ants in an ant heap.

In front of most of the houses in Haiphong, there are small red paper ribbons with drawings of grimacing faces on them. An old legend tells of two brothers who could spot demons even in broad daylight and drive them away. So Heaven entrusted them with the mission of barring the way to the evil spirits which are in such terror of the brothers that to this day, even their pictures on the red

paper ribbons send them flying. To my way of thinking
the people of Viet Nam should have hung these wonder
working ribbons all around their country. Then the
legendary brothers might have barred the way to the
demons of Communism that now held the whole upper
half of the country in their strangling grip.

Looking at that refugee-overrun city, you didn't have
to be a doctor to know that it was rotten ripe for an out-
break of typhus, smallpox, cholera and other plagues.
The members of the Preventive Medicine Unit said little
about it; words were unnecessary.

Depending on your nature, you either yielded to a
sense of helplessness or you plunged into work, to reduce
the suffering even a little and so help to save an edge of
dignity for Man.

Obviously the first problem was to house the refugees
somehow. There were perhaps 150,000 of them at the
moment, living in the most squalid conditions, sprawling
all over the city streets and gutters. There was no sanitation of any kind. The refugees were living under shelters
they had improvised from rice mats, cloth or plastic rain
covers.

You can't build a refugee camp in the middle of a city;
therefore we looked around on the outskirts. Most of
those outskirts were made up of rice paddies or bogs
along the edges of the Red River. At last we found a
reasonably dry spot about four miles from town, on the
road leading from Hanoi into Haiphong. "Highway" in
Viet Nam means a barely navigable road. At this time,
our site was about forty miles from the Bamboo Curtain,
which gave us a little elbow room.

But under the terms of the Geneva treaty, the small

crescent-shaped "free" area around Hanoi and Haiphong was destined to shrink on successive dates. By October 11, the town of Haiphong would be swallowed, bringing the outposts of Communism within fifteen miles of us; and in January the Curtain would be visible from the camp itself. On May 19th, 1955 the entire area north of the 17th parallel was scheduled to be in the hands of the Viet Minh.

Many unkind things have been said about the slow way in which the cogs of American agencies move. But within a few days after he had been informed of our plans, Mike Adler, head of the U.S. Foreign Operations Administration (USOM) in Haiphong, had 400 large tents flown in for us from Japan. "Army Sixty-Man Tents" they were called; for us they often sheltered 120 people or more.

The French Union Forces lent us some Moroccan soldiers to set up the tents and we found a few hundred coolies to help them. The design of the camp was there in Dr. Amberson's sketch. He was the brain of this project and we were his hands. I was learning how to build tent camps.

After several days of work, the first camp was completed. The tents were arranged in twelve rows. All told we set up 149 tents, with a broad roadway through the middle of the camp. An elaborate set of drainage ditches kept the place from floating away during the monsoon season, though the ditches did form something of an obstacle course. If you didn't walk with one eye on the ground, you were liable to find yourself knee-deep in a ditch.

Certain broad paddies around the camp were used as

latrines. I pulled a few prize boners, which Dr. Amberson caught in time, like locating the latrine area on the windward side. About once a month we would spray these fields with a strong insecticide solution. Later, in some of the other camps, we dug Marine-type slit and straddle trenches to be used as toilets.

The colony was scarcely a pretty sight to the eyes and certainly no treat to the nose. Nevertheless we were pleased, even elated. A beginning had been made. The first row of tents I reserved for my hospital area: a tent for sick call, a nursery for new-born babies, a couple of supply tents and five or six tents for sick patients. I also set aside tents for the elders or mandarins who would act as camp leaders.

We had one large tent in which we stored rice and straw mats. The rice had a scent all its own (boll weevils, I believe), while the straw mats had a musty odor, especially during the monsoon season. The canvas had a scent and the pungent insecticides we used had theirs. Corpsmen Baker and Harris had a pet baboon, Jasmine, who made her home in this tent too. Blend all these aromas together and add the draft from the washrooms and you will see why visitors never had much trouble in locating our headquarters.

We christened our first camp "Refugee Camp de la Pagode." The name sounded Oriental and melodious, and it didn't worry us that the area was fresh out of Pagodas.

This was just the first camp. There were others to come: Camp Cement, Camp Shell, Camp Lach Tray, Jardin des Enfants, to mention only a few. We had to move fairly often when the mud would no longer support us, or when the Red frontier came too close for comfort, or once when we were driven out by rats, the four-legged kind. Like old circus hands, my small staff and volunteer refugees were soon adept in tearing 'em down and putting 'em up.

A Mr. Mai Van Ham, the Head of the Vietnamese Evacuation Committee, became one of my best friends. He gave me everything I asked for, from extra coolies to some understanding of the Oriental mind. He was often at odds with the French, sometimes even with an impatient American doctor. Once in a while we almost came to blows, but the situation would always straighten itself out when we both realized that, each in his own way, we were trying to do our best for the oppressed people of Viet Nam.

Now we began to round up the refugees and move them in with us. In the medical tent we held daily sick call. Here, with our American medicines, we saw three or four hundred refugees a day. Respiratory diseases were common, as were trachoma, worm infestations, fungus infections, and tuberculosis. These were just everyday run-of-the-mill complaints. Every corpsman I ever had could soon recognize a case of yaws at ten feet.

The Navy supplied our unit with every piece of machinery, a truck, water tanks, a jeep and insecticides. But it didn't seem quite fair to the Navy that we should ask it, officially, for soap, vitamin pills, dressings and aspirin for the hundreds of thousands of people who passed through our camp.

During the months of August through October, we acquired most of our pharmacy for the camp's sick call through that time-honored, slightly irregular custom known as "cumshaw." My corpsmen and I would take turns running out to the bay in boats or hitchhiking on the Commodore's helicopter. Any nearby U.S. ship was our goal. We would bum a dozen bottles of vitamins, half a dozen vials of penicillin, a handful of Band-aids, some antibiotics—anything they were willing to give us. In this way, through the generosity of the Navy, unbeknownst to the Navy, we collected an impressive arsenal of drugs.

In return for these gifts to cumshaw we gave lectures to the crew on just what was happening, we described what most of the refugees had to endure in order to escape from the Communists. We often carried a large plastic-covered map of French Indo-China to illustrate our talks.

Anyway we kept our pharmacy stocked. But by December most of the ships had left and only four or five transports remained. We couldn't keep going back to them, so we thought up a new system.

I wrote home for medicines. Terramycin was the most important drug, so I wrote first to the Pfizer Laboratories in Brooklyn, N.Y. I told them of our job, of our people, our camp and our problems. I even sent them some photos. I asked for a "small contribution"—say, 25,000 capsules—of terramycin.

The Pfizer Company sent 50,000 capsules! Later they contributed other drugs—penicillin and streptomycin. The total commercial value must have run into tens of thousands of dollars. Its real value to us was incalculable.

There were other good samaritans. Mead-Johnson sent many gallons of liquid vitamin preparation; Pan American Airways gave us 10,000 bars of soap, and other companies contributed many other things. That's the way the "decadent capitalistic system of America" responded to our S.O.S.

And we never lost a single opportunity to tell the refugees that such fabulous charity could only be found in a country which allows companies to grow large and rich. And with every one of the thousands of capsules of terramycin and with every dose of vitamins on a baby's tongue, we said these words: *"Dai La My-Quoc Vien Tro."* That means: This is American Aid.

Every person I asked for help responded wholeheartedly. That gave me a wonderful feeling. It was as if all the wealth of America were in my own medicine chest. All I had to do was reach and ask, and reach and ask I did. Camp de la Pagode became a corner drugstore. About all we lacked were comic books and ice cream.

At Camp de la Pagode we had to process our water. Our aim was a gallon per refugee per day and sometimes this amounted to 12,000 gallons. If medals could be awarded to machines, I would recommend the highest honors for our water-purifying equipment. The water was drawn from a rice paddy, passed through a sand filter and two chemical feed tanks, and finally through a chlorination gizmo before passing into the big 3,000-gallon rubber storage tanks. This was *nouc my* (American water) and the refugees drank it with obvious distaste. They much preferred the typhoid flavor of the water in certain forbidden paddies.

The particular paddy from which our water was lifted had to be barbed-wired off because the refugees would wash their feet, food, and livestock in it. One morning all the water in that rice paddy was black. We looked into the matter and found that the cause was a vegetable dye which a peasant had used to color her clothes for the summer Viet Nam fashions. She had simply dumped the concentrated solution into the rice paddy when she was finished with it. We had to put the whole camp on water rations until the stuff had cleared.

One day I heard more than the usual uproar of screaming and yelling at the water plant. I went over to see what was up. I discovered that two of my corpsmen, Norman Baker and Edward Maugre, had decided that the water sediment tanks needed cleaning. So they had simply taken six of the Vietnamese children, had removed their clothes and had thrown them into the tank, waist deep in water. Then they handed them brushes and soap and told them to scrub the bottom and side walls. The children loved their job, and the corpsmen ended by having to fight a small war to keep the rest of the children in the camp from climbing into the tank and joining the soapy six.

Our first refugee camp became the center of attraction for visiting VIP's. We took all our visiting firemen on usually muddy tours of the usually very muddy camp. The Governor of Viet Nam came almost every week and tramped through the camp speaking to his people and lifting their hearts and their spirits. The Mayor of the city of Haiphong, a simple man and a fine one, was another guest who came often.

But sometimes we had less well-loved visitors. These were the Viet Minh Communist agents who made daily trips to the camp. The refugees were the first to point a finger of suspicion at them: "There is a man in Camp de la Pagode, Tent 5-B, who is saying that we should go back home immediately to fight for the true nationalists, the Viet Minh. He is very strange this one." Every couple of days the police would find such agents.

The people of Haiphong came out in their rickshaws to have a look at us and see if living conditions might perhaps be better than those in town. I am sure that many of them moved out to this new housing project.

Vietnamese Public Health, who were themselves desperately short-handed, gave us some native nurses whenever they possibly could. Like all the natives, these girls were so eager to escape into the safety of the south that none of them stayed with us very long. So we would take some of the cleaner-looking refugees and persuade them to stay on in the camp a month or two, instead of the usual ten days. We would teach them to wash their hands and other basic things; they learned quickly and were always anxious to help. Then we "crowned" them "nurses." So along with running a camp, being interpreters, father-confessors, American images, doctors, corpsmen, water-plant operators and the like, we also served as professors of a school of nursing.

After a few weeks the camp was going full force and we were a thriving little community all our own. We had our own name; we had our own government; we had our own hospital, complete with corpsmen and black-toothed, betel-chewing nurses; and we had our own groceries. The daily ration was six hundred grams of rice, very carefully weighed, a couple of fish, and such extras as happened to be available.

I have left for the last the most important center in the camp, our church. It was not a great and noble structure —just another tent with its sides rolled up. There was a

wooden altar there, and the Blessed Sacrament was reserved by day and night. Every morning at dawn, Mass
was said for the camp's fifteen thousand inmates. I feel
sure God heard the prayers of those poor refugees. They
asked no favors for themselves. They just thanked Him
with strong voices in prayer and in song. They thanked
Him for having given them their freedom.

And they turned to the Mother of God, to the Blessed
Virgin of Fatima, and said, "Remember, O most gracious
Virgin Mary, that never was it known that anyone who
fled to Thy protection, implored Thy help, or sought
Thy intercession has been left unaided, and we thank
Thee, O Queen of Queen of Queens."

CHAPTER THREE

Leading the Life of Dooley

New refugees came streaming into the camp all the time, and although others were always being evacuated, our camp population was usually around 15,000. Our first jobs were to delouse, vaccinate, and inoculate, and to screen out all those who had communicable diseases. But there was more to it than that. At the sick call tent I was now seeing between three and four hundred patients a day, all of them desperately in need of medical treatment. What was I to do? Should I leave them in the camp to die? Should I send them back behind the Bamboo Curtain?

There is a motto in every service that says (approximately) that a man should keep his mouth shut and *never* volunteer for anything. Happily that is a rule Americans talk about but seldom observe when things get tough. And I guess I have a special habit of sticking my neck out.

Captain Amberson was worried at the way I kept on increasing the work load of the camps. I argued that the spraying and vaccinating that was being done in the

15

towns was haphazard and dangerous; therefore no one should be allowed aboard any ship unless they had first been properly processed by us. Now I brought the Captain another headache.

"Doctor," I said, "rules are rules but we've got to do something for these sick people. We can't just surrender a woman and child to the Communists because the kid happens to have smallpox. We've got to treat the smallpox so that the family can get aboard a ship."

Captain Amberson looked at me in a tired way. But I could see that he understood and that as a doctor he agreed with me. He just felt sorry for a young eager-beaver who thought he could lick every problem in sight.

"All right, Dooley," he said, "treat the smallpox. You know the limitations as well as I do. Go ahead and do the best you can."

So, in addition to the delousing, vaccination, and camp sanitation, we took on the job of curing the sick. This at least doubled the size of the medical effort. We stepped up sick call and I enlarged my hospital tent for surgery.

And then, quite suddenly, Captain Amberson was called to Washington, D.C. Commander Sidney Britten, who replaced him, was a lab man from way back. Where Captain Amberson's main interest had been in field work, such as teaching JG's how to build refugee camps, Doctor Britten's main interest was in epidemiology. He took over the lab at the old French Navy base and left sick call and the running of the camp pretty much to me.

In October, Commander Britten had to return to Japan. He took with him most of the corpsmen and I was left alone with Dennis Shepard, a new arrival, Peter

Kessey, who was superb, and noble Norman Baker who was to be with me to the bitter end. Now a Naval Medical Officer of one year's vintage was in sole command of the medical division of the refugee camp. In theory I was subject to my superiors, but in practice I was left almost wholly to my own devices. By guess and by God, I kept the unit running for the eight months that were left.

Every day I expected new brass to arrive and take over. But no one came. Much later I heard what had happened. Captain Amberson had reported that the situation in Haiphong was extremely dangerous and that the fewer men we had ashore the better: "Young Dooley has the situation well in hand and can carry on."

Sure enough, in mid-November orders came through naming me as "Commander, Task Unit 90.8.6.1." The decimal points showed that I was far down the line, but I was pretty proud anyway. Then some joker decided that for security reasons our mission would be known as Operation Cockroach!

Call it what you like, my job kept me working fifteen or sixteen hours a day. Reveille for Dr. Dooley and his small band was 5:00 A.M. I shaved in a basin of cold water, brushed my teeth in chlorinated water brought from the camp, and dressed, all in a matter of minutes. My standard working clothes—and every day was a working day—consisted of khaki trousers or shorts, a T-shirt and a uniform shirt with the sleeves cut off.

Never did I neglect to wear my collar insignia and my Navy hat. These, especially the hat, were important. Symbols mean a lot in the Orient. To the hundreds of thousands of people who passed through my hands, the bars on my collar and the eagle on my hat stood for authority, true, but also for friendship and for that whole far-off nation called the United States. My corpsmen and I were determined to make these people understand that what we were doing for them was being done because of the love and generosity of the American people.

"The gloves on your hands are good," a refugee was likely to say, "but the eagle on your cap is bad." Communist propaganda had been hard at work. It had confused these simple people so that they scarcely knew friends from enemies.

"No," I would answer, "the eagle on my cap is good. The eagle stands for America. America sends the Navy, which brings you the American Navy doctor. And it is the American Navy itself which is going to take you to safety in Saigon."

There were lots of these arguments every day during sick call. Sometimes I couldn't help wishing that it would be possible just to work without talking. But this was a job that had to be done.

Almost always I would find one or two boys sleeping in the corridor outside my door and a few more sprawled in my jeep. There would be a few of these "little Dooleys," as people called them, at my heels when I appeared, at a little after five, either at the camp or in the village church for Mass.

After Mass, breakfast. For this I usually went back to my quarters, where I made instant coffee on a hotplate and drank it, with crackers.

By six o'clock or a little later, I was in the Medical Tent for the day's first assortment of tropical ailments, fractured limbs and wounds that were infected and oozed pus. The patients queued up before my arrival, and there was always still a line by the time I knocked off for lunch.

By one o'clock I tried to be back in my tent for the serious business of learning Vietnamese. My teacher was the mandarin who was Chief of the Camp. I felt it was important for me to be able to talk directly to my patients, even if I didn't speak correctly. Thank goodness Vietnamese is a very easy language. After a couple of months I was able to speak as well as I needed to. I could even sing a few Vietnamese songs.

At three, when the temperature dropped to a bearable 100 degrees or so, I went back to sick call. And no matter how long the lines were, I had somehow to crowd in a visit to the hospital tents for checking, treatments, and sometimes surgery. This carried me to 5:30 or 6:00 P.M., at which time I got into my jeep and drove to other areas where our people were quartered. This included a warehouse in town which housed thousands of them.

For dinner I often went out to an orphanage run by Madame Vu Thi Ngai where I acted as the Orphanage Medical Department. By eight or thereabouts, I was back in my room for a cold sponging and bed. There was always a prayer in my heart that I might be allowed to sleep through until morning. But often my young guardian angels would have to wake me up. Someone had taken a turn for the worse or some new atrocity victim had reached our camp and was in need of patching.

This was the basic pattern. With minor variations it was the life I led from the end of August till the middle of May. It melted off a good third of the 180 pounds I had arrived with. The grind went on in spite of several bouts of malaria, four different types of intestinal worms, and a mild but uncomfortable case of acne. My hands were always dyed red, because I did not have much alcohol to use as a cleansing solution but did have plenty of tincture of merthiolate. After I finally left Viet Nam, it took me a whole week to bring my hands back to near normal.

The drain on my energies never bothered me much. I was young and strong and was a sound sleeper. There were other strains that were harder to manage. Try as I would, I could not keep from being saddened by the sorrow and savagery I saw all around me. My conscience kept driving me to do more and more, and the stabs of guilt reminded me that I could never do enough.

Toward the end of my assignment, I seldom went out any more to the ships in the bay. It was a four hour trip by small boat. With the Viet Minh itching for trouble, our launches made no trips after dark. And during the day I was too busy to go. But the lure of a hot shower and a decent meal sometimes were more than I could resist. Once I succumbed to the lure, and sent a message, via my walkie-talkie, requesting the command ship's helicopter.

When the skipper asked me what was up, I answered boldly "Sir, I am in desperate need of a hot bath and a decent meal." He merely chuckled.

Soon the whole task force knew about Dooley's bathing difficulties. They had all heard about the time I went aboard the flagship and was invited to have lunch in Admiral Sabin's cabin.

I was wearing a battered khaki shirt and trousers, my hands were as usual stained red with merthiolate, and I needed a bath badly. Nevertheless, with all those high-ranking officers present, the Admiral seated me at the foot of the long table, directly facing him. I was very much flattered but he brought me up short.

"Don't get any ideas, doctor," the Admiral said, "You just smell so bad I want you as far away as possible."

But soon the time came when my heart was so heavy that I grabbed at anything that was good for a laugh. I even began to look kindly on Baker's clownish pet baboon, in spite of the fact that he was chewing the seat cover off our truck.

CHAPTER FOUR

The Power of Propaganda

Often in the early evening when the day's work was done, I would go to the tents with the mandarin chief and talk with the people who had just escaped from the Communist zone. The escapees were as much interested in me as I was in them. I used to ask them what their life had been like under the Viet Minh rule.

In these talks I learned a lot about the people of North Viet Nam and how they had come under the heel of Communist oppression. And after a while I could understand the confusion in their minds and in their nation. The present is always born out of the past. So in order to know what made these people think and feel as they did today, I did a little boning up on their yesterday.

I found that not so long ago, Laos, Cambodia, and Viet Nam, independent nations, were combined to form a country known as Indo-China. In the 1860's and 1870's France had gained domination and the countries were a French colony until August, 1954. There was a small intermission in this French rule between 1940 and 1945, when France was forced to yield her colony to Japan. But there was never a real struggle and all during World War II, France managed to do "business as usual" with Indo-China through a provisional government she set up to protect her interests. Then in 1945, Viet Nam, Laos and Cambodia were liberated. Not by the French, however, but by the British and Americans.

At this time a man who had become well-known and much-loved as a worker in the underground during the Japanese occupation, came to the fore. He said: "We have gained our independence from the Japanese and I see no reason why we should yield it again to France. We are a strong nation; we will be our own rulers." A great many of the people looked up to him as their leader and he set himself up in Hanoi as president of the new republic. This man was Ho Chi Minh, which means Ho, the Enlightened One.

The French sent Ho into exile but on December 19, 1946, his forces started a war for independence, started it with tortures and atrocities. While many Americans condemned Ho's methods, they sympathized with his goal. They felt that he was a patriotic Vietnamese nationalist. All over Asia nationalists of this type were winning the struggle against the colonial powers. Ho Chi Minh's forces were called the Viet Minh.

But in 1949, after the Communists had conquered China, Ho suddenly revealed himself in his true colors by proclaiming the Democratic Republic of Viet Nam, which was promptly recognized by the U.S.S.R., Communist China and the other satellite states of the Soviet bloc. The world now learned that Ho Chi Minh had been a Moscow-trained puppet from the start.

The war between France and the forces under Ho Chi

Minh dragged on for eight years. From 1949 on, the United States supplied military and economic aid to France in the struggle to save Viet Nam from the Communists. But in May, 1954, the French were defeated at Dien Bien Phu and the war came to an end.

Then came the Geneva treaty dividing Viet Nam at the 17th Parallel, the northern half, with a population of about thirteen million, going to the Communists while the southern half, with about eleven million, was to be ruled by the National government in Saigon. It is interesting to know that Viet Nam, herself, the country which was divided, did not even sign the treaty which divided her. John Foster Dulles, the Secretary of State who represented the United States at Geneva, walked out of the conference. He said that the United States would not sign the treaty because we would not be a party to an agreement that handed half a country over to totalitarian tyranny.

One of the important clauses of the Geneva Treaty stated that anyone living in one zone who wished to go to the other was not only to be *allowed* to move but was to be *assisted* in his journey for a certain period of time— until May 1955. A mixed neutral commission, composed of representatives from Canada, Poland and India was created to supervise the evacuation; this commission was also instructed to do everything possible to make the exchange of people between the north and south easier.

What neither the French nor the Communists, let alone the Americans, had foreseen, was that so many people would elect to give up everything they possessed to live out their lives in the Free World. In Viet Nam a proud and noble race paid a staggering price in human misery for the issue of freedom.

In the early months the refugees simply floated down the river's many tributaries, into Haiphong. But before long, the Viet Minh decided that too many people were fleeing their country and they took measures to slow down the exodus. They tightened their controls until escape became more and more difficult. But still these brave people would not give in. They set sail from their coasts in little sampans that were not built for the bold winds of the South China Seas. Often the adventure turned out to be a desperate one; often it ended in tragedy.

The French Navy was always on the alert to help any escapees that succeeded in reaching the waters along the free enclave. Because the refugees were always sheltered in our camp while they waited for transport to the south, I was usually kept informed of any rescue operation that was going on. This was a great help to me at the camp because it gave me warning of what to expect.

Early one morning Captain Gerald Cauvin of the French Navy, who was in charge of these rescue operations, sent a man to our camp to take me to the French Navy pier. He said he had just received a radio message from a French seaplane that fourteen large junks had reached the Baie d'Along.

Cauvin was sending down a French craft, an LSM, to meet the junks and bring them to Haiphong. I alerted the camp to expect five hundred or so very sick people (actually there were more than eleven hundred). Then Captain Cauvin and I went aboard the LSM and sailed four hours down the river to the bay. The seaplane that had spotted the refugees had meanwhile returned to Haiphong.

We arrived in the bay about noon. It was absolutely silent, this strange place with its bare rocks jutting high, no foliage, no vegetation, just barren grey stones.

The sampans had sailed into the bay, one behind the other. They were huddled together. Several of the boats were lashed end to end. As we headed toward them, we observed them closely through our binoculars. The brilliant noonday sun on the clear water made this a storybook fairyland, but what he saw was hardly a storybook sight.

Jammed on to these fourteen sampans were more than a thousand refugees who had sailed an unbelievable two hundred miles in the rough South China Seas. They had done this in small fishing junks, risking all dangers, against all odds, accomplishing the near impossible. Though they were in the warm sun, they were drenched and cold. The sea had made them so deathly sick that they had vomited their stomachs dry. Even from a distance you could see that the coldness of the night had made them stiff in every joint and ache in every bone. They moved around the sampans helping each other, yet in the mass they seemed immobile, sprawled over the wooden decks.

The constant soaking in salt water during all hours of the day and night had made their skins dry and the blazing sun had cracked it. Their feet had been wet so long that their ankles were swollen and bloated. All of them looked sick and miserable.

When our LSM was close enough for the refugees to make out the French flag on our stern, a heart-warming thing happened. Recognizing us as friends, they hoisted their own drenched flag on a broken spar. It was a flag they had hidden for years—their emblem, their symbol.

To the top of their highest mast they hauled the Papal banner, a yellow and gold flag on which were the Pope's tiara and the keys of Saint Peter.

As we pulled alongside, eager French hands reached down to help these people into the well-deck of the LSM. Most of the refugees were transferred to our ship. Some of the healthier men were left aboard a few of the sampans, which were lashed to the sides of the LSM. We headed back to Haiphong with our load.

Meanwhile we handed out tea, water and French rolls to the escapees. Though there wasn't enough food to go round, it helped. The little LSM with a crew of only two dozen, did not carry large food stocks. I wished I had remembered to bring along some sacks of rice.

Cauvin and I found several elders who seemed to be the leaders of the party. We took them to the cabin and asked: "Where did you sail from? What was life like in your village? Who are you?"

The old men sipped their strong tea and their wrinkled, haggard faces were at once sad and hopeful, as they told their story in tired voices:

"Cua Lo is our village. It is about 300 kilometers south of here, on the sea coast. It was a happy village years ago. Our landscape is flat. It is divided into many small rice paddies that are often green with rice crops. During the monsoon the grey sky is alive with scudding clouds but during the hot season the sun shines all the time and the sky is blue. Our people worked in the fields all day, irrigating their crops and plowing up the red brown mud behind squelching water buffalos.

"Others in our village were fishermen. The junks that brought us here belong to them. They are strong boats, with two masts and large mustard-colored sails. But they are not built to sail the open seas.

"In 1951 our enemies became our rulers. They forced us to accept a new set of laws and a new way of life—the Communist way of life. But the Communists don't call it that. They say it is Viet Minh Nationalism. It is all very confusing, even for us, the mandarins, who are supposed to be intelligent.

"The Communists are very clever. They know just how to handle the people. And they don't mind telling lies. They promised to take lands that had belonged to the rich people of the Colonial Power and divide that land among our own poor. And this was done. But very soon they taxed the poor so cruelly that at the end of the harvest their pocket money was less than it had been before.

"Another thing the Communists promised us was the water wheel. This was to be a great thing for us. You see, our land was divided into small paddies that were separated from each other by small mud dikes. At times a rice crop must be in water and at times it must be dry. So at various times the water must be transferred from one field to another. If the receiving field is lower than the other, there is not much difficulty. But if it is level or even higher, then the water has to be transferred by hand in buckets. This transfer goes on for hours and hours at a time, and it has been like that for centuries.

"Now Ho Chi Minh came and he said 'I will give you

a water wheel. And this will make your work easy. It will lift the water for you.' And he did give water wheels to thousands of farmers. But as the water wheels belonged to the state, he said it was only simple justice for the state to ask the farmer, as his end of the bargain, to pay the state a certain percentage of his crops. As you can imagine, that percentage was not small.

"They told us that our new way of life would be much better than the old way. But we are not so stupid. It did not take us long to see that the Communist plan was to sacrifice the present generation to the happiness of the one that is to come.

"We saw that the new land reforms produced only famine. Hunger clawed at our bellies. At first it seemed as if the new Viet Minh nationalism was going to bring us justice. But before long it showed itself in its true colors and we knew that that too was a lie. The Communists had lots of new-fangled economic theories. And the people of our village saw that they were to be sacrificed ruthlessly to these new ideas. Never before has there been such cruelty as we suffered under this new order.

"All of us had only one thought: we must escape. So for weeks we made our preparations. Every day we hid away small balls of rice, so that we would have something to eat on our journey. We dared not talk openly of escape since our village was run by a mandarin who, though he was an old friend of ours, had now become a Viet Minh commissar. The Communists had changed him into a cruel man. He stationed his agents everywhere, in the market place, in nearly every hut.

"We made our plans though, even if we could not hold meetings. For the new laws said that there could be no gatherings of more than four people. We passed the word to each other while we bent our backs in the rice fields, or while our fishermen unloaded their catch, or while our women visited with each other in the market place.

"Finally we were ready. Our plans—and our prayers—reached a climax. The night had come. There was no moon, the sky was dark and the seas were calm. From eleven o'clock until one the next morning, we slipped down to our boats singly or in twos. In the meantime a boy named Mai Van Thinh undertook to divert attention from us by singing loudly at one end of the village. The police, the Commissar and many soldiers went to see what was going on. This gave the rest of us a chance to get our junks loaded.

"The boats were built to handle only about twenty-five people each. That night each one of them carried a hundred. As quiet as the night itself, we slipped away from the shore and headed out into the South China Sea.

"Our escape was a success. But we were not happy; our thoughts were with Mai. Sooner or later we knew that his part in our escape would become known. Then what would be his fate? Mai's father and mother had been killed in the war and his only brother, Cham, had been burned alive, for no other reason that we could see except that he was head of a Christian youth movement. Would Mai have to endure the same fate?

"Using both oars and sails, we headed straight out to the open sea. We were anxious to get beyond the three mile limit as quickly as possible. We wanted to reach international waters. By morning we were out of sight of land; we felt a little safer. That is, we were safe from one danger, although now we had the sea to struggle with.

"Our plan was to sail north. But we had no compass nor was there anyone amongst us who knew much about navigation. However we managed to turn so as to put the morning sun on our right hand. We headed for Haiphong because we knew the French and Americans would help us. We knew that they would take us the rest of the way to Saigon . . . and freedom.

"Our trip lasted five days and five nights. We could not have fires, for our wood was too wet. We were forced to eat our rice when it was damp and soggy. Our tea was soaked with salt and so it only made us sicker. We had little or no drinking water. The decks of our small junks were splashed by every wave that came along. It was terrible.

"But early this morning we found ourselves in a strange place and we knew we must have reached our goal: Baie d'Along. When we saw your big seaplane we were sure. And now we are free. . . ."

The mandarins had come to the end of their story. And now from the well-deck of our LSM, we heard a soft chanting. The refugees were singing a hymn. We all went out on deck to listen. I could not make out all the Vietnamese words. The mandarins hummed with the song, then translated it into French for us.

The people were offering their thanks to God because He had helped them during this great crisis in their lives. They chanted: "O Lord, we love the beauty of Thy house and the place where Thy glory dwells. Provide that our days be spent in peace with Thee."

CHAPTER FIVE

The Orphanage of Madame Ngai

There was a certain monotony in our life in Viet Nam. Day after day, week after week, month after month, we saw the same diseases, the same terrible misery. We faced the same shortages of materials, the same lack of help.

Worst of all, we had the same feeling of being unable even to scratch the surface of the tragedy all around us. Combine this with the little personal discomforts, the lack of hot water and clean clothes, the blistering heat, the constant sweating, the need always to speak in a foreign language—and you get some idea of the effort it took to live each day.

There was no place to go and forget about it, no place to put your feet on the table and read the funny papers. If we did knock off for an afternoon, a sense of guilt would hit us and the afternoon's pleasure would be gone.

But there was always one highlight in our Haiphong life. This was the orphanage of Madame Vu Thi Ngai, the orphanage of An Lac.

In time this orphanage and its hundreds of smiling

children became *our* orphanage and *our* children. We really sort of adopted them. And they adopted us. Madame Ngai was the head of the place and my corpsmen and I became the Orphanage Medical Department. The U.S. Navy became the Orphanage Trust Fund.

Madame Ngai was a proud Tonkinese woman who had once been rich. She was good to look at, with jet black hair, white teeth, and lovely olive skin. Her eyes were broad and wide, with that intriguing Oriental slant. Madame Ngai was large. It was as if she needed room for a big heart so that she could love all the children who were in her care.

In all of Viet Nam, there was only one other person who was as charming as Madame Ngai, and that was one of her wards, little Lia. Lia was seven years old and she was as delicate and pretty as a doll. There was only one thing wrong with Lia: she had one leg and where the other had been she had only a short stump. Her right leg had been blown off at the thigh when she stepped on a land mine in 1954 near the town of Phuly. The explosion made her an orphan as well as a cripple.

For a right leg, Lia used a wooden crutch. I met her when I first went to the orphanage in August. After some time, she let me look at her stump. It had healed poorly and there were raw surfaces on it even six months after the amputation. I asked Lia if she didn't want me to take care of the stump for her. She said she did, because she loved the *"Bac Sy My,"* the American doctor. So we started a little campaign. First I did a little minor surgery, then Lia followed my instructions. She stretched the muscles, exercised the stump, soaked it, kept the dressings on and kept it clean. As a result she had a good functional stump by Christmas.

Next I wrote to the A. S. Aloe Company of St. Louis, told them Lia's story and asked them to help. Although they themselves could not supply the artificial limb I had asked for, they got in touch with a man in New Jersey and arranged for him to make a new leg. They told me the measurements they needed and I sent the information along. And so a limb was made that was just right for this little girl, a limb that could be adjusted to her growing. Some time later, it arrived in Haiphong.

Lia now had a new leg, an American leg. Her eyes glowed when she put it on and walked with it for the first time. She cried and smiled and then cried again (and so did Madame Ngai, and so did Baker, and so, I confess, did I!). Gratitude spilled out of Lia's eyes, until she couldn't say thanks—and didn't have to. Lia loved her leg so much that she even slept with it on. When we asked her not to, she was puzzled. She did not take off her Vietnamese leg when she slept, she said, so why must she take off her American leg.

Another child we all loved very much was Nguyen. We never knew his last name. Madame Ngai said she found him when he was four, in the village of Thai Binh. Nguyen was now six. He had a wonderful smile and a loving face and tuberculosis of the spine. He was a hunchback. It was hard for him to walk, so he waddled. He could not sit down comfortably, so he would lie down to eat his meals. When he laughed very hard, which he did very often, he would fall to the ground on his back and roll. Nothing could stop him from keeping up with the others. Sometimes we would take the orphanage children to visit one of the American ships, where they would be given an American type party. On these occasions Nguyen was by all odds the best man about the ship. I think he had a collection of some fifteen sailor hats which were given to him or, more often, swiped by him.

There was a two year old child whose name I don't remember. He had had trachoma infections in both eyes when he was a baby, and now at the age of two, he was totally blind. If he had had medical care during infancy, he would now be able to see.

There were other children who had deformities of one kind or another. Some were really pitiful to behold, even for a case-hardened doctor. And almost all the children had seen death in hideous forms, had felt its shock and its terror. They had watched villages being burned and fields destroyed. But in spite of everything they still smiled, and they loved, and they made life good and complete for the rest of us.

The way Madame Ngai would thank those of us who were lucky enough to be able to help her, was to invite us over for dinner. It was always a true Vietnamese dinner: batwing soup, rice, of course, in all its forms, fish heads, chickens served with the head on, raw pork with sauces, an oil made from decaying fish, salad—where from, O Lord, and how well washed—and other foods which were, surprisingly enough, pretty tasty even to American palates.

During dinner we would squat on our haunches or sit on pillows. Buddhist joss sticks always smoldered in colored jars of sand. At one of these parties we asked Madame Ngai to tell us how the orphanage was born.

Where did she find all these children? Where did she get the money to feed them? Who were they?

This was Madame Ngai's story: "In 1946, in the village of Thanh Hoa in southern Tonkin, there were many great battles. Families were split. Dead littered the village. Children were left on the roadside to die alongside the bodies of their parents. Wars do not have time to take care of babies.

"I lived in Thanh Hoa. In fact at one time my family was the richest of all in the canton. I had a lovely large house with many *mau* of fields around it. Although much of my house was destroyed in battle, I was still able to live there. I went along the roadways and took the children who were still alive, and brought them from the ditches to my house. My servants and I took care of them. "But when another battle started in Thanh Hoa, we knew we would have to escape. So I left with my children. There was now six hundred of them.

"When Nam Dinh fell to the Viet Minh in 1949, I was forced to move again, only by this time I had a thousand children to take with me. Five times I had to repeat those moves until, finally, I settled here in Haiphong.

"The mayor of the city gave me a fine building to house my children and the city helped to support them. But at the beginning of this year, the year of Dien Bien Phu, the French needed my building for a hospital, so I had to move to the house we occupy now. I should be ashamed to entertain you in such a common house, and yet it is my home, and so I am not ashamed. This is how I came to be the mother of a thousand children."

The funds Madame Ngai used to run her orphanage were her own or were acquired mysteriously. The clothes

she gave the children were sometimes those she was able
to charm from some French Admiral or General. For
instance she persuaded Admiral Querville, the com-
manding officer of the French Navy to donate some of his
surplus uniforms. These were then cut up and down and
made into small suits for the children.

The orphanage was prospering. Madame Ngai loved
every child and smothered them all with great tenderness and devotion. Her children were all good and well-
behaved little Buddhists.

The Americans entered her life in August of 1954
when the small landing force arrived in Haiphong to
set up the funnel's mouth for the evacuation of refugees.
My boss, Dr. Amberson, and I were on hand too. It did
not take long for Madame Ngai to find us—or perhaps
for us to find Madame Ngai.

Madame Ngai had only met one other American before we came along, a flier downed during the Japanese
occupation whom she had hidden in her home. Although
she spoke wonderful French, the only words she knew
in English were "Yes, thank you very much." When we
told her she should have a little more variety in English
conversation, she would smile and say in French, "There
is no need to say anything else."

When Captain Amberson left Haiphong, his last words
to me were, "Don't neglect the kids at Madame Ngai's."
That was one of Captain Amberson's orders that Dooley
tried to obey to the letter.

Often when a U.S. ship would come up the river we
would ask the Captain if he would allow us to throw
a children's party. If the answer was "Yes," at two o'clock
in the afternoon we would pile thirty or forty children

into a truck, drive them to a pier and load them on a crash boat which would take them out to the ship. They would have comic movies, then cookies and ice cream. And after the movies and the banquet, the children would entertain the sailors. They would sing Vietnamese folk songs or do ancient Tonkin dances. The older boys would demonstrate judo.

Whenever they could do anything to help us, the orphanage children were ready. On the mornings we loaded the refugees at the pier for the trip south, Madame Ngai would come and bring half a dozen of the older children. They would help the refugee children of Viet Nam to carry their bundles and sometimes they would carry the refugee children themselves. They would help the mothers with their baskets and their balance poles. Madame Ngai would pass out bread to the refugees, bread that had been bought with American Aid money and cut up to make small sandwiches. While I was in Haiphong, Madame Ngai and Madame Querville distributed more than 700,000 loaves of bread to embarking refugees. And that is a lot of loaves in any language.

When was the orphanage going south? We kept raising the question, fearing that Madame Ngai and the children might be trapped. "Not yet! Not Yet!" she would answer week after week. There were still new children coming into her home who needed her. She would hold on until the last minute.

By the middle of April, however, there were Communist riots in the city, and Madame Ngai at long last made up her mind that the time had come to move on. So, in the middle of April, the orphanage moved,—beds, mats, planking, pierced steel plating used for floors, desks, bassinets, barrels of chopsticks and rice bowls, small sewing machines, coolie hats, blankets, rice, vitamin pills, artificial leg, ping-pong table and everything else.

Admiral Querville personally supervised proceedings when they went aboard an LSM early in the morning and, before the sun rose over the Red River, the children were on their way down to the bay to be transferred to the General Brewster for their Passage to Freedom. Baker went south with the orphans to make sure they were well treated on all sides. After the two day, three night voyage, they arrived in Saigon and were taken to their new home. Meanwhile Madame Ngai's "American orphans" in Haiphong sighed with relief for her sake—and suddenly felt very lonely.

CHAPTER SIX

Communist Re-education

The children of Viet Nam become old very young. They are mature and grave while still in their early teens and they are often very brave.

There were the shoeshine boys, for instance, who roamed the streets of Haiphong like cattle. In a way they were just little tramps, accomplished thieves, but they were good little tramps and good thieves. They shined my rough combat boots, the inside out leather type. They rubbed and spat and grinned, and did it again. I would ask them, *"Ong di nam khomp?"* "Are you going to become a refugee and leave this Communist land?" "Yes," they would reply, "We are going south sometime."

These kids couldn't quite get out the absurd word "Dooley." So they called me *"Bac Sy My,"* which meant "American Doctor." Sometimes these young "tramps" acted as a junior intelligence network. And when someone once called them "little Dooleys," I was flattered.

Then there were the children who worked for us in

the camps. Some of them stayed with us for months. They did adult work, accepted adult responsibilities; when they could bum cigarettes, they even smoked like adults. Yet they were only eight, or ten, or twelve years old.

Each of my corpsmen had six or seven such young assistants. Their badge of honor was a white sailor hat. A gang of them followed me around day and night, sometimes to my embarrassment. They might come to lead me to a feeble old woman who could not leave her tent, or take me to see a man who was crippled. They ran errands for me, fetched things I wanted, boiled water for the sick call tent. Sometimes they did my laundry but as they were very apt to wash the clothes in the *wrong* rice paddy, I discouraged that activity. And sometimes they would ride my truck just for the fun of it, as children should.

Whenever a Vietnamese official wanted to see me, he would spot one of these kids with the sailor hats, or one of the shoeshine boys, and tell him to find the *"Bac Sy My."*

When one of my young assistants left for the south, we held a little ceremony. Various ships' officers had given me their ensign bars. So on the official day, the Lieutenant would commission his assistant as an "Ensign in the U.S. Navy." A bar was pinned on him and his sense of self-importance increased so you could notice it. I hope the Personnel Department of the Navy will be understanding when it hears about my unusual recruiting service.

The Viet Minh aimed much of their propaganda at the children and teenagers of the nation, and they went to horrible lengths to make their propaganda stick. The first time I ever saw the results of a Communist "re-education" class was during the month of December.

The Communists had set up their controls in the village of Haiduong. One day they visited the village schoolhouse and hauled seven children out of their class and into the courtyard. All of them were ordered to sit on the ground, and their hands and arms were tied behind their backs. Next they brought out one of the young teachers with hands also tied. Now a new class began.

In a voice that was loud enough to reach the children who were still in the classroom, the Viet Minh accused their prisoners of treason. A "patriot" had informed the police that this teacher was holding classes secretly, at night, and that the subject of these classes was *religion!* They had even been teaching the catechism!

Because the seven had listened to the teachings of this instructor, the Viet Minh accused them of "conspiring against the state." As a punishment they were to be deprived of their hearing. Never again would they be able to listen to the teachings of evil men.

Two Viet Minh guards advanced on each child and one of them firmly grasped the head between his hands. The other then rammed a wooden chopstick into each ear. He jammed it in with all his force. The stick split the ear canal wide and tore the ear drum. The shrieking of the children was heard all over the village.

As for the teacher, he must be prevented from teaching again. Having been forced to witness the atrocity performed on his pupils, he endured an even more frightful one himself. One soldier held his head while another grasped the victim's tongue with a pair of pliers and pulled it far out. A third guard sawed off the tip of the teacher's tongue with his bayonet. Blood spurted into the man's mouth and gushed from his nostrils on to the ground. He could not scream: blood ran into his throat.

Yet neither the teacher nor any of the pupils died.

The victims were brought to us and we treated them as well as we could, though this was not very well. We did prevent infection; penicillin took care of this. But nothing we could do could give those children back their hearing.

I know that it is not just to judge a whole system from the conduct of a few. But this was Communism to me. And from December until the last day, there were two or three atrocities every week that came within my personal orbit. I can hardly bear to think how many more must have taken place that I knew nothing about.

Under the Geneva agreement, anyone who wanted to leave the north had the right to do so. But from the day it was signed, the Communists violated this agreement. This so-called guarantee of free and unmolested passage became a farce and ours were probably the only camps in history that people had to escape *into*.

Because this flight into freedom took place in the face of a massive propaganda campaign that was reinforced with torture, it was all the more impressive.

From the very beginning the Communists bombarded their people with stories of the "imperialistic" French and Americans who "kidnapped Tonkinese citizens." Hour after hour, month after month, they hammered their falsehood home. And all young men and young women were forced to attend "re-education" classes every morning where the political commissars told them stories about the American barbarians.

To rice-paddy peasants, some of the stories sounded pretty plausible. Americans, they knew, were fanatics on the subject of cleanliness, so perhaps they did cut the hands off the people who vomit over their ships. America is a land of giant industrial power, so perhaps Americans do need coolies for slave labor. It fits the picture so well; probably it's true enough.

Of course in order to make propaganda stick, the victims must never be allowed to hear a breath of truth. So the Bamboo Curtain was clamped down tight on North Viet Nam. One voice, however, did succeed in piercing the Bamboo Curtain. The refugees told me of secret battery radios that were smuggled into them. On these they listened to The Voice of America. In this way they learned of the evacuation and of the promises made at Geneva.

But even though the propaganda campaign did not prevent thousands of people from trying to escape, it did succeed in sowing seeds of doubt and suspicion. When they first arrived at our camps, the refugees eyed us cautiously, and sometimes even with active dislike. They were probably thinking, "Look at that sailor the young doctor calls Baker. See him going around with that spraying machine on his back. What deviltry is he up to? Probably he is spraying diseases over us."

I was not the only one who felt this fear and suspicion in our escapees. All my corpsmen felt it too.

As the people had been told that we would inject diseases into them if they came to our camps, vaccination was a real problem. American bacteriological warfare! We were reported to be carrying out large-scale medical experiments for which we were using the people of North Viet Nam as guinea pigs.

Often the refugees were so suspicious of us that it was hard to get them to come into the sick call tent for treatment. So we would hold sick call in *front* of the tent. Then some ten thousand refugees would squat on their haunches all around us and observe. "What will he do?" they would ask each other. "Watch him". . . "Be careful."

And in spite of everything we could do, once in a while we did have riots, or near-riots in our camps. There was the first time we set up the compressed air motors and the DDT dusting machines. Ed Gleason, one of my corpsmen, was the boss of this operation. Dusting-gun in hand, he led the other corpsmen who were lined up behind him with six more dusting-guns. The idea was that as each refugee passed down the line, he would be given a good going-over with DDT to keep down louse-borne epidemics.

There were several small children in the first group. When they got alongside Ed, he pushed the trigger on his gun and swirls of dust flew down on the kids. Their mother had a long balance pole across her shoulders with a basket hanging on each end. When she saw this American blowing powder on her children (she had been told of this particular American atrocity), she went after Ed, swinging that pole like everything.

After a blow or two, Ed managed to get his arms around her, polka fashion, and the chief mandarin and his men helped to break up the fight. Then Ed dusted the other corpsmen thoroughly to prove that this powder was harmless.

I took a beating or two myself. One day a woman

brought me a baby whose body was covered with ulcers. Yaws and ulcers respond miraculously to penicillin and this looked like a routine case. I gave the infant a shot and told the mother to bring it back the next day.

A few hours later, I heard shouts and curses, and saw the woman holding the baby aloft for the people to see. Here was proof that I was an American monster! The child had reacted to the penicillin with an angry-looking, though quite harmless, case of hives. The terrified mother was in no mood for explanations. She handed the baby to a bystander, grabbed a good, stout stick and called up a dozen sympathizers. When Baker rescued me at last, I had broken ribs, black eyes and assorted bruises.

The next day, remembering the importance of face in the Orient, I went to the woman's tent alone and unarmed. Luckily, as I had expected, the hives had disappeared and the horrible ulcers were healing nicely. When she saw me, the woman burst into tears, fell at my feet and begged for forgiveness. She stayed in the camp for weeks and served as one of my helpers at sick call. And she was always eager to exhibit her nice clean baby. The effect on the other refugees was worth a few fractured ribs to me.

In the end however it was our "miracle drugs" that were the great persuaders. I had never thought much about the power of antibiotics, vitamins, soap, cleanliness and the rest of it. Now I know that they have power unbridled.

The Communists stopped at nothing to prevent their people from escaping into the Free World. They used trickery, threats, violence and even murder, to stop the southward rush. They made it illegal for more than one member of a family to travel on a bus or train in the affected area at the same time; or for more than two people to go on foot together on the roads that lead to the evacuation zone. This made it hard for would-be-refugees with large families to break away.

To by-pass this rule, desperate parents often sent their children ahead, two today, two tomorrow, with instructions to go to the American camp and wait for them there. I saw youngsters by the dozens, by the hundreds, arrive all alone, exhausted and sorrowful, as they settled down on the fringes of my camp to wait for their parents. Often they waited in vain.

In many parts of North Viet Nam the Communists ruled that special passports would be required. Not to leave the country (that would have defied Geneva too crudely), but just to cross from one canton into another. To get a passport you had to pay steep fees and the red tape involved was fantastic. But you could not travel as a family group unless you owned one of these passports.

Having at long last managed to get a passport, a family might set out on foot on the long road to Haiphong. Fifteen or sixteen days later, their food almost gone, foot-sore and perhaps sick, they would arrive at last at the canton line. There they would run into the old dodge of the expired passport.

The Communist guard would examine the hard-won document and laugh. "Comrades, don't you know? This passport is only good for fourteen days. Oh, you can't read? Well, anyhow, you've got to go back and get a new one."

As a leftover of the war, many roads were sown with mines and booby traps. The Communists dug them up.

But very often they did not detonate them. Instead they tossed them into rice paddies, swamps and bushes close to the line of our evacuation area. Many citizens were blown to bits trying to crawl to freedom at night.

Yet the Geneva treaty states very clearly. "Any civilians residing in a district controlled by one party who wish to go and live in the zone assigned to the other party shall be *permitted and helped to do so* by the authorities in that district." The italics are mine.

CHAPTER SEVEN

The Dying City

The months passed and still the refugees continued to pour in week after week from all the provinces of North Indo-China. Some days we would get fewer than a hundred; others days there would be thousands. They came by boat, by land, by foot, by junks and sampans.

Camp de la Pagode was taken down in March and other camps were erected. During January and February we had three huge camps with a total capacity of over 30,000. Eventually all of my Navy corpsmen left except the dauntless Norman Baker.

Norman Baker, Aviation Boatswain's Mate, Third Class is first class in my book, or maybe first class plus. He was sent to me early in the game as, of all things, my French interpreter. The person who sent him did not know that my facility in French was one of the reasons I had been chosen for this job in the first place.

Baker and I had decided that it was not up to us to set matters straight. "All right, so I won't interpret," he said, "but I think I can be useful in other ways." That was the understatement of the year.

49

It was at a luncheon given by Admiral Sabin that I made a clean breast of the Baker affair. "You see, sir," I said, "I speak French and now I speak Vietnamese, so I don't need an interpreter. But Baker is a wonderful assistant. So I've been holding on to him under false pretenses, I am afraid."

The admiral put on a mock-serious look. "Well, well, I hate to disappoint you, but you didn't fool us. I knew all along that you were pulling a fast one."

It turned out that there were a lot of other fast ones he hadn't minded either. Some people had complained about my habit of lifting supplies from the ships in our area: "Look what Dooley's done now—sixty drums of oil, and he just signed his name for it! Who the devil does that boy think he is?"

"Well," the Admiral would say, "I'm sure he wouldn't have taken the stuff if he hadn't needed it urgently."

Many months after our talk, I received a letter from Admiral Sabin commending me on having been awarded the Legion of Merit. "The Book says the Lord will help those who help themselves," he wrote, "and it seems to me that, in the evacuation of Indo-China, you, Dr. Dooley, several times managed to give the Lord a nudge."

Not once did the Admiral fail to endorse my nudging. I had superb support, and without it I would have been licked.

I should like to take time out for a moment here to say an official thank you to the Navy. When they first came to us the refugees associated only terror with a uniform. But they soon learned to associate help and love with our work. I wanted them to know that our love and help came to them because we were in the uniforms of the

U.S. Navy. The reason we were there to help them was because we were in the service. That is why Baker always saluted me and called me *"Quan Hi,"* which means Lieutenant, rather than doctor. We had come with ships to take them to freedom, with medical aid to heal their ills and bind up their wounds, with large supplies of lifesaving drugs freely donated by American firms. I felt that it was important for those refugees to know that although we had come late to Viet Nam, we had brought not bombs and guns, but help and love.

By April the push began to slow up. It was clear that the new masters of Viet Nam had succeeded at last in plugging up most of the remaining holes in their Curtain. The French Army was almost gone, along with its equipment, quonset huts, tanks and office furniture. Only a few hundred French soldiers were still encamped on the finger-like projection that was Haiphong. Operation Cockroach, my end of the more elegantly named Passage to Freedom, was entering its final stage. Once, when a helicopter was sent from a ship for me, the Communists were already so choking close that the plane had to land on a small lot in town.

Haiphong, the city we had known, was dying. Every day more shops and houses were deserted. Only a few vehicles remained of the heavy motor traffic we had found when we arrived. The bazaar had been burned "by accident." There was little doubt that it was the work of Viet Minh infiltrators.

By now my evenings were spent either at the camps talking to the refugees or in town at the abandoned bank building where Major John McGowan, the U.S. Army

Military Attaché, and I would try to scare away our loneliness by talking.

All the city people who intended to leave were either leaving or had already left. By this time, most of those remaining in the city could be assumed to be pro-Viet Minh, if not actually full-fledged Communists. It was now that the real trouble began.

The Governor's staff and the Mayor's staff had left, with only skeleton crews remaining. All was grim and silent on the streets. Violence was common in this "new society" that was trying to settle itself on the ruins of Haiphong. The first riot exploded in the second week of April.

It seems that several hundred Viet Minh trucks had arrived with so-called refugees piled high in back. These refugees did not want to live in the camps; they wanted to move into the city, where there were hundreds of empty buildings.

As the truck tried to drive across the bridge that lead to the city, the French stopped them, saying that the Viet Minh were not scheduled to take over Haiphong completely until May 19th, and that this was beating the Geneva deadline. The occupants of the truck insisted that they were refugees and could therefore enter the city at any time.

Tempers flared on both sides. The bogus refugees pushed across the bridge and the French soldiers poured out tear gas bombs. Hand to hand fights developed. Several of the "refugees" were killed, hundreds were wounded, including many soldiers; and the Red radio broadcasters in Hanoi had had themselves another propaganda holiday. Such clashes became more and more frequent.

It seemed to me that the time had come when the shoeshine boys must go. I consoled them by telling them that the shoeshine business was certain to be lush in Saigon and that a good thief finds it hard to survive in a police state.

What finally convinced them, I think, was the matter of shoes. The idea came to me in a flash one day. "Well," I said, "you might as well throw those kits away. There will be no more shoeshining when the Viet Minh arrive. Or do you think you can shine canvas shoes?"

That did it. They looked at me suspiciously, and then at one another. I wasn't kidding. From the frequent forays behind the Bamboo Curtain, they knew that canvas sneakers were what was worn among the well-dressed Viet Minh.

At that point they agreed to be vaccinated and dusted with DDT. One April morning, Baker and I boosted a few of them into a truck and went down town to gather up the rest from the street corners. We gave each of them a loaf of bread and a final delousing and watched them shoulder their shoeshine kits and file sullenly aboard the landing craft. They arrived safely in Saigon, and I'm sure that city hasn't been the same since.

On May 10th, the Viet Minh staged another proof that the American doctor and Americans in general were hated by the people of Haiphong. Our green truck was stolen. It was a one-ton truck Dr. Amberson had gotten from the Haiphong Public Health people. They had originally received it from the French, who in their turn had gotten it from the U.S.A. through American Aid.

I used it for ten months, for every kind of mission. It had been turned on its side in a riot and, in another demonstration, had had all its windows broken. The spare tire, the cap of the gasoline tank, the windshield and the light bulbs were missing towards the end. The monsoon rains had done their best to make it mouldy. You couldn't sit down in it with clean trousers and come out looking the same. Yet the little chariot could go any-where, haul anything, and was well known all over the city. To make sure that no one forgot it, a big American Aid insignia was painted on its side.

On the 10th of May it was stolen from a parking space near the bank building. Late that night we found its charred and blackened chassis in the town square. The Viet Minh had apparently burned it in a public demon-stration to show the Americans that they were despised and to show the Vietnamese that the new Democratic Republic of Viet Minh was going to have nothing to do with anything that was "made in the U.S.A."

The Catholic Mission was now about empty. The nuns, the school children and all the priests except one very old native had been sent south. I hated to see them go; they had become good friends. They were made with hearts of that proverbial precious metal and they had been wonderful to all of us Americans. Father Felice had offered early Mass every morning in the Mission Church, usually full of barefoot chanting natives. He told me he usually knew when I arrived because my boots squeaked as I made my way to the very front row.

The old native priest who was left in charge would say Mass until Haiphong fell. He intended to try to continue even after the Viet Minh took over. He knew that he might be made to suffer but he said that he was old and that a martyr's crown might ensure his entry into Heaven. Haiphong's last weeks found his Masses attended by a dwindling handful of the devout.

On the 4th of May, in accordance with the terms of the Geneva treaty, an advance contingent, the Viet Minh Committee of Experts, was allowed to enter the city. The idea was that they would go to the City Hall, the Governor's office, the public utilities plants and so on, so as to learn how to take over from the Vietnamese, the last of whom was scheduled to leave on the 16th of May on the last boat out. Thus water and electricity would be in working order and the turnover of the city would be smooth.

The Committee arrived, 480 strong, in brand new Russian-made Molotova trucks. They were dressed in high-collared grey uniforms, pith helmets and canvas shoes. Most of them spoke French very well.

They stopped me about four times daily, when I was trying to cross the street, or drive out to the camp or go down to the docks. But they were always polite and respectful. They said I was the only American they had ever met who could speak their language. Why had I learned it? Did I intend to stay on and try to help the "true people of Viet Nam" when the new Democratic Republic established its offices? I said that my job was about over and that I expected to leave soon.

They sent a delegation out to the camp. "When you treat people in America," the leader argued, "do you make any difference between Democrats and Republicans?"

"Certainly not!" I said.

"Very well then. You must not make any difference here between capitalistic dupes and the loyal people of Viet Minh."

With that he ordered his men to divide up my drugs and my surgical supplies—half for me and half for the Democratic Republic of Viet Nam. And there wasn't a thing I could do about it.

I tried to be polite to the newcomers, but perhaps I only gave them the impression that I was afraid of them. And I was. I was afraid all the time that they would lock me up somewhere and hold me for "investigation." Investigations can stretch out for years in Communist states, as many an American knows to his cost. And there were only four of us Americans in the whole of North Viet Nam.

The coming of the Committee of Experts would not have been so bad in itself. But they brought several thousand armed bodyguards with them who raised hell in the city. Riots, fires, "spontaneous" anti-foreign demonstrations and beatings of old men and women who had been friendly to us became common. The newcomers blamed all these things on the French.

There was a riot in front of the City Jail and the Committee of Experts demanded that all prisoners be freed at once. The French said they would be freed on the 16th of May, according to the agreement, and not until then. That set off a "demonstration" that ended up in tear gas and firing on the crowd.

One afternoon I climbed up in the steeple of the Mission and looked all around the city. You could see little puffs and clouds of smoke in seven or eight parts of town. The smoke meant that demonstrations were being

The row of medical tents which was my first "hospital."

Floods, and the epidemics they bring, were a constant danger. Luckily we had none during our year there.

Two of my best nurses.

This is what childhood is like in a land devastated by the Communists.

Vietnamese children eat American rice.

Skin infections were very common in a land where soap was a rarity.

Bone infection, in an advanced stage; education could have prevented this.

Christmas Day, 1954: a party at Madame Ngai's orphanage.

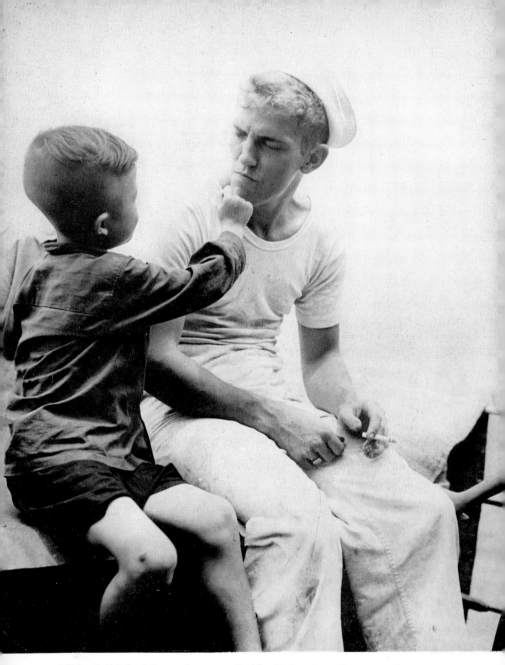

This child had been just as afraid of the Americans as the next one.
Would you believe it now?

Our house in Vang Vieng: hardly elegant, but functional, clean, and in keeping with the rest of the village.

Jeep call.

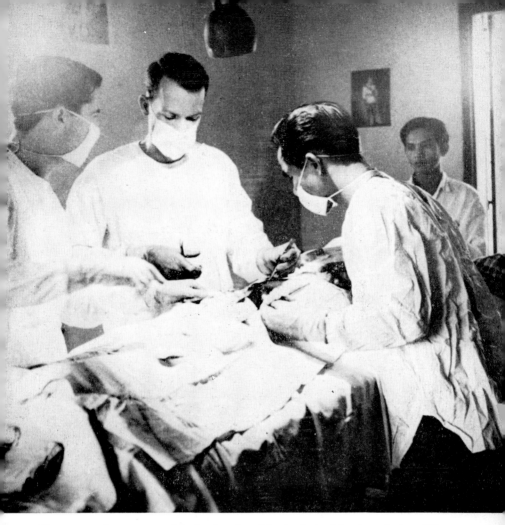

Our operating room, with the local *médecin indochinois* assisting. The little generator did double duty for this and for the movies.

This young boy was carried down the mountains and through the jungles for several days. It was the lad's left leg which was infected; the right had atrophied from disuse.

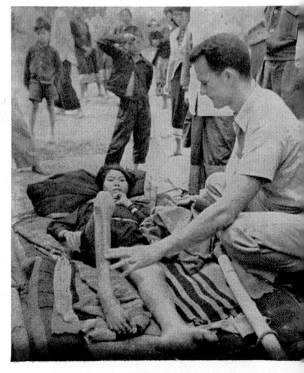

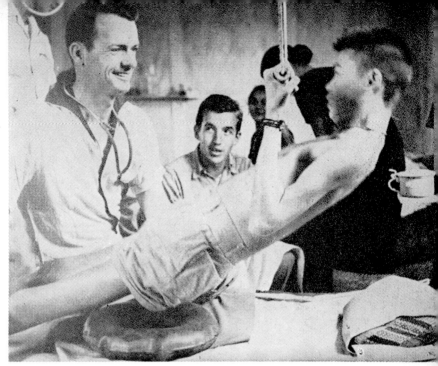

Jack Lartz for USIS

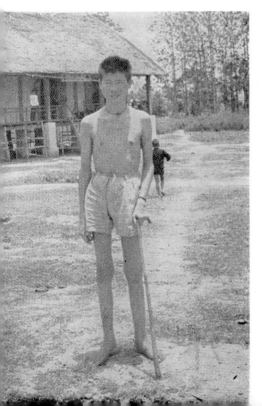

So he was put to bed in an outfit constructed by John De Vitry. Shortly after surgery he started exercise and improved daily. Soon he was up and walking. A little later he was helping around the hospital, and finally returned to his village on foot.

Norman Baker with a very dead jungle prowler. That's Chai at the left
with his hands on his hips.

Erica Anderson

Unloading some recently received Pfizer drugs.

Erica Anderson

Part of our Lao student staff.

Erica Anderson

Payment for a day's labor.

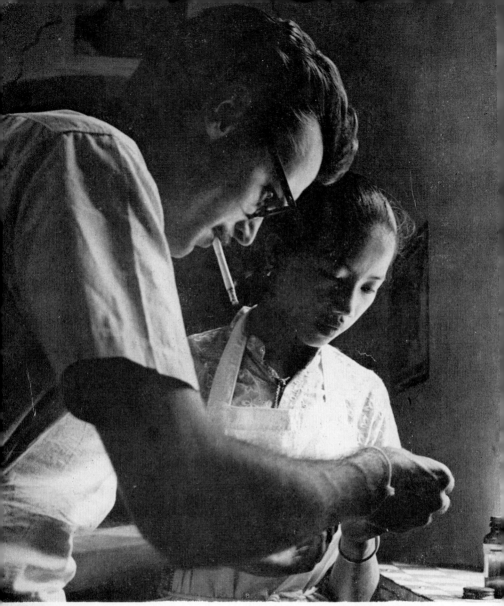

Erica Anderson

Dwight Davis and a student. Teaching is perhaps our most important job in Muong Sing.

broken up with tear gas. The French used it often because it was the least violent method of dispersing a mob.

The French forces did a good job during those last weeks at keeping some semblance of order. I spent most of my time dodging riots, driving blocks out of my way to get to my objective in order to avoid being stopped and questioned. A good deal of the time I spent just being afraid.

By the 10th of May, we had taken down the tents of our camps and moved the last remaining refugees into empty buildings in the city. It was on the 12th of May that I saw my last atrocity.

By this time the Viet Minh were in legal possession of all but a very small area on one side of Haiphong; illegally they held just about all of it. You could see them everywhere you went. They patrolled the main streets and waterways, and at every street intersection their sentries stood guard. They captured a young Vietnamese boy. He was the wild type. And he still wanted to escape from Viet Minh territory and dared to try.

He ducked through the back streets across the line of demarcation, known as the Demilitarized Zone. Here the Viets caught him. They formed a circle around him and beat on his feet with the butts of their rifles. They kept up this torture until their victim collapsed, then they added more blows for good measure, all on the feet and ankles. This was to serve as an example to future runaways!

When the boy regained his senses, he discovered that he was alone and that the road had been abandoned. He managed to drag himself into a nearby alley. There a rickshaw driver found him and somehow smuggled him across to us on the free side.

I had no X-ray equipment but I could see that the damage was beyond repair. The boy's feet and ankles felt like moist bags of marbles and gangrene had already set in. I did the best I could. We managed to get the boy into a crash boat which took him out to a French LSM that was waiting to sail for the south. He would be crippled for life, but at least he was free.

Our last loading day was set for the 12th of May. It was a dry, hot morning. The shuffling of thousands of bare feet made the dust rise off the ground at the loading area. You could taste that dust. The only sound you could hear was the chugging of the LST motors. We were still spraying the refugees with DDT.

This was the last day of the last loading. Some 3,600 refugees were huddled together on the decks with their cloth bags, their balance poles at each end of which dangled their household possessions, the babies on their mothers' hips. They were a desolate slice of humanity. They walked slowly in line to be dusted with DDT, to accept a loaf of bread, or perhaps a few diapers and a small bag of clothing. But for me they were much more than a mere mass of wretchedness. I had seen their courage and their undefeated hearts. During all those bitter months, I had come very close to these people. Their tragic fate and their gallant dream of a life in freedom had become my dream too. They were my suffering brothers.

What we had *done* in Haiphong seemed much less important to me than what we had *learned* there. I had seen simple, tender, loving care—the crudest kind of medicine inexpertly handled by mere boys—change a people's

fear and hatred into friendship and understanding. I
had seen it translate the "brotherhood of man" from a
mere phrase into the sort of practical reality that plain
people can understand.

"I must remember the things I have seen," I said to
myself, "I must keep them fresh in my memory. I must
make myself see them again and again in my mind's eye;
I must live through them again and again in my
thoughts."

The last LCT pulled away from the dock. The boat
headed down river as an enormous sun sank blazing into
the quiet river. Operation Cockroach had come to an
end.

Soon I, too, would be saying goodbye to Viet Nam.
But I knew that I could never leave behind me the things
I had seen. To me that experience had been like the
white light of revelation. I had come to know what it
meant to be a doctor; and I was proud of my calling.

I started back to the deserted camp. The heat was
intense and I choked over the dust that floated like a
gritty fog over this Asian world. I walked slowly, my feet
keeping time to some lines of Robert Frost's that had
been echoing and re-echoing through my mind during
these last harried days:

> "The woods are lovely, dark and deep.
> But I have promises to keep,
> And miles to go before I sleep,
> And miles to go before I sleep."

CHAPTER EIGHT

Home Again

I had left the death of North Viet Nam in May of 1955. A few more months of duty in Japan, then my resignation from the Navy and soon it was February 1956. I had already been home a couple of months. But I could not forget the half million, dirty, mutilated, heroic people of Viet Nam and their gallant fight to live in freedom. I had only one wish: to go back to Southeast Asia as soon as I possibly could. But so far I had not found the way to keep the promise I made to myself on that afternoon in Haiphong nine months earlier.

All I had been able to do since I was back in America was to talk! I preached so much that my family and friends began to worry. "Look, Dooley," they said, "you've had adventure enough. When are you going to settle down?" My mother kept reminding me of all the things I had always wanted and now might have: a home, a wife, kids, a nice medical practice, maybe a few fine hunting horses. Even my old professor at medical school got into the act. I had always wanted to be a good orthopedic surgeon. Now he told me that if I wanted to succeed in my ambition, I had better get on with my postgraduate training.

How could I make these people understand that things

could never be the same for me again? They had not seen what I had seen. With my own eyes I had witnessed the enormous power of medical aid in all its Christlike simplicity. Besides, I knew that the future of the world might be won—or lost—in Southeast Asia.

And there was something else. Something that Dr. Schweitzer calls the fellowship of pain. We were to talk of this when I had the good fortune to visit him in 1957. I had responded, as everyone does, to the immense wisdom and the immense love of this dedicated man. Dr. Schweitzer believes that everyone, all over the world, who has learned from experience what physical pain is, belongs to a special company. And in this brotherhood of the anguished come all those who are related to sufferers. And whom does not this include?

In a very small way, because of my profession, I believed that I had found entrance into this Fellowship. The suffering people of Southeast Asia, the "have-nots" of the world, needed help. Somehow I must find a way to bring it to them. But how?

Then one evening I was asked to a dinner at the Vietnamese Embassy in Washington. I had a sudden feeling that my hope of returning to Indo-China with a medical team would be decided by what happened at that dinner.

I knew that I would not be allowed to go back to Viet Nam, for the whole north was now locked behind the Bamboo Curtain. I was not needed in the south, where the medical teams of the Filipinos' Operation Brotherhood were already doing a wonderful job. But Laos offered a perfect field for the kind of work I could do. I wanted to go to Laos.

At that dinner besides my good friend the Viet Nam

Ambassador, there were also present some diplomats from Cambodia and Laos. All evening I kept talking about the kind of medical mission I had in mind—small, privately financed (mostly out of my own pocket), without any government or church sponsorship or obligations. As I saw it, the team would consist only of myself and a few of the young Americans.

We would be plain Americans working among the plain people of the country, wherever we were needed. It would be a simple example of cooperation on a people-to-people basis.

The Cambodians listened politely. But the Ambassador from Laos was really interested.

"But, Dr. Dooley," he said at last, "why should you, a young man just released from your naval duty, with a career before you, choose to make a sacrifice like this? You have a lot to offer. But what do you stand to gain?"

I tried to tell him how I felt. I said that it seemed to me that medical aid, offered on a people-to-people basis could do a lot to join the people of the West and the people of the East in a true friendship. Since I had served in Southeast Asia and had seen the need for this kind of help, I felt that it was my duty to go. And I was young, unattached, free to go whenever and wherever I was needed.

I talked and talked but the Ambassador didn't seem convinced. Then suddenly I remembered something that big, hard-boiled Boatswain's Mate Norman Baker had once said in answer to the same kind of question.

I translated Baker's words into French as well as I could: "We just want to do what we can for people who ain't got it so good!"

That did it. The Laotian Ambassador beamed. "Dr. Dooley," he said, "my country would be honored to receive your mission. Will you come to see me at the Embassy in the morning?"

I was there ahead of time. The Ambassador gave me a thorough briefing. He told me why medical teams like mine were needed in Laos. He said that for the whole population of the country, about two million people, Laos had only *one* doctor who would be recognized as a medical graduate by western standards. I couldn't hide my surprise and he looked at me and smiled a sad smile.

"Oh, we have a few men we call *médecins indochinois*," he said, "but they are only graduates from the lycée who have had a couple of more years in medical training. (A lycée is about equal to an American junior high school.) But for the vast majority of our sick people there are only the witch doctors and the sorceress. You will find everything in my country difficult, possibly dangerous."

I said we were willing to take our chances, but I also promised to be careful. The Ambassador shook my hand warmly and told me that he had confidence in me.

"Many times before," he said, "white men have come to help us. But always before they had other motives: colonization, trade, even our religious conversion. But I really believe that your motive is a purely human one. That will make your mission unique in my country." Then, he added with a twinkle in his eye, "And also, for some of my people, a little hard to believe."

I started making my preparations immediately. First I got the International Rescue Committee to take us under their wing and give us a sort of official status. Then I took another look at my bank account and said a prayer.

I had been salting away the proceeds from my book and lecture tour. Now, with my hat in my hand, I made the rounds of the drug companies and the surgical supply houses.

Their response was generous beyond my wildest dreams. I received over $100,000 worth of antibiotics, a good supply of surgical dressings and bandages, surgical instruments and equipment, a huge supply of vitamins and protein extract, a very welcome check, and from Walt Disney, a sound projector as well as a collection of movies for the children of Laos.

It is wonderful to see what a good cause can produce in the way of human kindness. In New York, just to take one instance, I went to Abercrombie & Fitch and ordered a lot of essential equipment: cookstoves, lanterns, sleeping bags, etc. The bill was staggering. When the salesmen learned the nature of my mission, he excused himself and disappeared into a vice president's office. He came back with the bill slashed to a fraction of the original amount. In Washington, while I was waiting to testify at a hearing of the International Rescue Committee, a woman sat down beside me and whispered, "Has Dr. Dooley given his speech yet? I have been chasing that man halfway around the country. I want to give him five thousand pounds of protein." The woman was Miss Florence Rose of the Meals For Millions Foundation. The five thousand pounds of multi-purpose food they gave me was directly responsible for saving hundreds of lives in my mountain hospital the following year.

Nor did the U.S. Navy let me down. They agreed to transport the tons of medicines, food and equipment we needed, even though I was now a civilian. And CARE donated about fifty midwife kits. Later in my story you will learn the good use to which these were put.

But I still had to line up the men who were to work with me. All along I had been counting on Norman Baker, Peter Kessey and Dennis Shepard, the most devoted and dependable of the enlisted men who had been with me in North Viet Nam. But would they as civilians want to return to a part of Asia where they had seen so much misery? Denny Shepard was newly married and was taking his pre-med at the University of Oregon. Kessey was attending pharmacy school and Baker, also a bridegroom, was still in the Navy.

Peter and Denny answered my call promptly and with enthusiasm. Baker's ship was somewhere at sea; several weeks passed before I could get in touch with him. Then one day, in Washington, I received a long distance call from Baker in San Diego. When I told him about Operation Laos (that's what I had christened our new mission), his roar could be heard from coast to coast.

"What! Back to Indo-China? Are you crazy? Why, you slave-driving fool—sir—you couldn't pay me to go back to that hole! Besides my wife wouldn't stand for it!"

There was an awkward silence. I just let him simmer down. Then . . .

"Hello . . . you still there, Doc? Listen, you don't really *need me,* do you? What makes you think we can really do any good out there? And there's something you seem to have forgotten. (hearty chuckle) Little Old Baker is still the pride and joy of Uncle Sam's Navy!"

I told him that I needed him, that Operation Laos was a tremendous challenge, and that I was pretty sure I could get him out of the Navy on an early discharge. I could hear his grumbles and moans.

"Aw, okay, Doc, sure I *volunteer!* But Priscilla's going to divorce me for this, sure as shootin'!"

(Bless her heart, Priscilla Baker did nothing of the sort. She went right ahead with a project I didn't know about at the time—having their baby.)

In July, 1956 I was on my way back to Asia. My men were to follow and meet me in the Philippines. I had to make a few stops on the way to give some lectures and to talk with the founders of Operation Brotherhood. The whole idea of non-sectarian medical service to foreign nations began with them. They gave me a whole lot of advice that turned out to be important for my mission.

On a sweltering day in August, I stood in the Manila airport watching a plane glide down through the heat haze rising in the runway. It taxied to a stop and the door swung open. Out stepped Pete Kessey, our lean and hungry-looking Texan, followed by 200-pound, barrel-chested Baker (flexing his muscles as always), and then quiet, serious Denny Shepard.

We had about an hour's wait before leaving for Saigon, our "staging area." The boys shot questions at me. "What kind of gear did we have? Where did we go from Saigon? What kind of place was Laos?" ("Yeah, man," Baker groaned, "I can see now that this means living on C-rations and holding twenty-four-hour sick call!")

Aboard the plane, I got out my map and told the boys that we would operate up north in the province of Nam Tha. Oden Meeker, who had served in Laos with CARE during the famine of 1954, had said that this was a critical area. It was the most isolated part of Laos, inhabited by mountain people who had rarely seen a white man. According to Oden, they were just ripe for the Communist treatment.

The boys listened solemnly. Then Baker said, "Look, Doc, you've got to level with us. What are the odds on this set-up?"

"Well," I said, "the odds are about standard for that part of the world. No better, no worse. We've all been in tough spots before, and we've done our jobs and come through . . ."

Baker hooted. "Oh, sure we did—only you forget that last time we had the U.S. Navy back of us!"

I switched to the kind of job we had to do. This time we wouldn't be so much "showing the flag" as showing "American face" to a lot of Asians who had been told that American white men were irresponsible at best. I asked them to remember what we had learned in Haiphong and try to think of what we could accomplish by working among people on the village level in Nam Tha.

But when we got to Vientiane, the capital of Laos, I found that I would have to change my plans. I had a talk with Dr. Oudom Souvannavong, the Minister of Health and the only doctor of medicine in Laos.

"Tell me, *mon docteur*," he asked suspiciously, "why have you really come to Laos?"

For the next ten minutes he questioned me sharply. At first I was flabbergasted, then I struggled to keep my Irish temper under control. At last, he began to smile again. Apparently he was satisfied that I was neither a spy nor a Jesuit in disguise.

He knew that I was interested in the north and, while

he did not actually forbid my going to Nam Tha, he warned me of the difficulties I would find in that Himalayan outpost. "There are many hazards there," he said, "isolation, the dangers of border life, Communist banditry, the fury of the monsoon rains, lack of transportation and a primitive people who do not know the white man and are sometimes hostile to him."

But when he had cleared his conscience, the Minister smiled at me. "Frankly, *mon docteur*," he said, "it pleases me greatly that you are willing to take your medicine to these most wretched of our people. You have our complete approval. But I must first ask you to get the approval of the American Ambassador."

That approval proved to be impossible to get. Ambassador J. Graham Parsons wanted my team to stay far away from the China border. The political situation in Laos was touchy; conditions in the north might become explosive any moment. He did not actually forbid my going to Nam Tha, but he would not give his approval.

So that was that!

I asked Ambassador Parsons where he thought my team might operate. He went over to the map and pointed to an area around Vang Vieng, about 120 miles north of the capital but still far south of the China border. During the Indo-China war, he said, Vang Vieng had been captured by the Communists; conditions were still pretty bad.

When I went back to the Ministry of Health and told Dr. Oudom that Nam Tha was out and that we wanted to go to Vang Vieng now, he agreed with Ambassador Parsons' decision. He said health conditions were terrible at Vang Vieng. The town had a medical station, but no doctor, nurse, drugs or equipment.

"You can perform a real service in Vang Vieng," he assured me.

So Vang Vieng it was.

Back at the Hotel we held a council of war. This change of plans was going to cut deeply into my bank account. Most of our equipment was designed for the mountainous north, rather than for the jungles and lowlands of Vang Vieng. Even our drugs were meant primarily for diseases we would find up north.

To get away from our worries, the boys and I went sightseeing that night. Strolling through the city, we found a Laotian "love court" going on. We squatted down in the audience and listened to the unique entertainment. It is sheer poetry, improvised on the spot. The boy praises the beauty, grace and virtue of the girl he is courting; the girl sings of the boy's nobility, charm, and bravery; and the audience applauds them with an enthusiasm that Americans reserve for touchdowns at home.

But I did not come only for the entertainment. I had something else on my mind. We needed an interpreter, a dependable man or boy who could understand the various Lao dialects and could translate into French.

Squatting in the love court audience, I began the search then and there. "What is this performance?" I asked loudly in French.

The people turned and stared at me. Then a voice said, "*Moi parler français, monsieur.*" He introduced himself as Chai, and translated the love poetry into passable French.

Chai was a graduate of the Vientiane lycée. I explained

that I was a doctor and that we were going to Vang Vieng and needed an interpreter. He accepted the job with enthusiasm and said that he knew all about Vang Vieng where he had *parentage,* which means relatives.

A few days later we piled into jeeps and started off on a reconnoitering trip to Vang Vieng, 120 miles north. I asked Chai if he knew the trail, *"Oui, mon docteur."* Later I discovered that Chai was not a liar. He just did not know how to say no.

For the next five hours, under a blazing sun, we crept and crawled through dense jungle, plowed through monsoon mud, and hit some long stretches of suffocating dust. But we also saw some of the most beautiful scenery on earth.

When we reached the Nam Lick River, we parked the jeeps, shucked our clothes, and were soon splashing in the green water. Everyone, that is, but Chai. He sat forlornly on the river bank.

Baker went and had a long talk with the kid; he came back grinning from ear to ear.

"For Pete's sake, don't laugh, Doc," he said. "He can swim all right. But he just ain't been checked out by the phantom that runs the river."

I thought Baker must be kidding. But when I had dried myself and dressed, I sat down beside Chai and learned that it was all true. Buddhism in Laos has become mixed with an ancient form of animism.

"This phantom of Nam Lick has taken many lives," Chai told me very seriously. "But when we return to Vientiane I shall make an offering. After that I will be able to swim in the Nam Lick without fear."

Sure enough, a few days later Chai plunged into the

river and swam and splashed with the rest of us. He had gone to the Buddhist temple in Vientiane, made his offering, and had been "checked out" by the monk for swimming in the Nam Lick. Chai even had a sort of charm to protect him which he wore tied to his wrist with a cotton string.

We learned something else about Chai. He would not kill anything. What about fishing, a sport Chai loved? Wasn't this killing, we asked him. *"Non, mon docteur,* I merely take the fish out of water. If he dies that is not my fault."

Knowing Chai helped us to understand the other people of Laos. Though born a peasant, Chai had been educated in a lycée, spoke some French, and was brighter than average. If he was so bound by the world of spirits and phantoms, the ignorant people of the kingdom must be even more under their influence. What hurdles would this create for us, we wondered, in practicing medicine in Laos?

The next day we drove through the jungle until nightfall. For some hours we had not seen a sign of life, so that when at last we sighted the village of Vang Vieng, it seemed like a haven to us.

The village rests at the foot of walls of rock that rise two and three thousand feet into the sky. The tops of the mountains are covered with pine, and stubby trees grow out of the rock of the side walls at painful angles. The tributary of the great Mekong River winds around the mountains.

This broad river pays no attention to the road. At several places along the trail large bridges were needed and at hundreds of places smaller ones were necessary.

When the rains come these are all washed away, making the road unusable for six months of the year. And even during the dry season, which starts in September, the 120-mile trip from Vientiane to Vang Vieng took a good two days!

CHAPTER NINE

Sick Call at Vang Vieng

Thanks chiefly to a member of Chai's *parentage* whom the boys named Ojisan (Japanese for "old man"), about half the population of Vang Vieng were on hand to meet us when the trucks and jeeps of Operation Laos arrived in town. Ojisan had told them that we were white medicine men and that we were bringing powerful remedies to the people. So many of the women and children brought presents of flowers, cucumbers and oranges.

The Lao dispensary was at one end of the square directly across from the home of the mayor. It was a low, whitewashed building of three rooms. Since it had no living quarters, Ojisan gave us a house which he owned.

Norman Baker was our chief construction man, in the best Seabee tradition; and under his direction the boys set to work making the dispensary into a hospital. They swept, swabbed, disinfected, and then whitewashed. With the help of half a dozen coolies, we cleared the surrounding yard (which was to be our "reception room") of debris, cow dung, and heaps of foul dressings and bandages. Then we built a fence to keep out the wandering water buffalo.

When the medical supplies had been uncrated, the boys did a good job of converting the empty boxes into tables, benches and cabinets in which to store our drugs. Then we borrowed some cots from a local detachment of the Royal Lao army. When these had been deloused and repaired, we set them in one room. This was our ward.

Our living quarters gave us a little more trouble. Ojisan's house was a typical Lao hut. It perched six feet above ground on stout poles and was surrounded by a "porch." The dwelling could only be reached with the help of a steep ladder. We climbed up, took one look inside, and came out shuddering. The place was filthy.

The boys tore out everything inside the hut including the bamboo partition between the two rooms. They swept the ceiling clear of soot, cobwebs, and rats' nests, then went to work on the walls. When the whole place had been swept out, they hauled up buckets of river water, broke out boxes of soap powder and bleach, and swabbed the deck Navy style.

The villagers made us a present of some bamboo mats to cover the floors, and we laid out our bedrolls and hung up our mosquito netting. Then we moved in the packing crate bookcases, benches and tables, and placed two cots against the wall to serve as lounges. This was going to be our "living room."

We never announced sick call and we didn't need to. Only a few days after our arrival we were awakened one morning by sounds that were to become a familiar part of every dawn—the howls of sickly babies and the hacking coughs of tubercular mothers. Why wait in line at the hospital, when you can camp on the doctor's front porch!

I was overwhelmed by the terrible health conditions

we found in Vang Vieng. There were yaws, tuberculosis, pneumonia, malaria and leprosy. Many women had suffered injuries in childbirth. Never in the thousands of hours I had spent in planning the mission in Laos, had I anticipated the depth of misery in which we were going to have to work and eat and sleep and live. Never did anybody in the Washington briefings, in the Lao Embassy, or in the refugee camps of Viet Nam, give us any idea of what life would be like for us four Americans in the tropical jungles of central Laos. I was completely stunned by the conditions that existed in the village of Vang Vieng.

One morning at sick call a poor woman pushed a huge, smelly bundle of rags into my arms. I peeled away the layers of clothing and uncovered a baby about a year old. Its abdomen looked like an overblown balloon that was about to burst, the chest looked like a little bird cage. There was a tiny monkey face with wild, unseeing eyes. Kwashiorkor's disease! And this was only the first of countless cases we were to see in Laos.

The sad part is that this disease is not caused by infection but by simple ignorance. It is the result of faulty nourishment. The end result is death. But this is one illness than can be cured if it is caught in time. That night I told the boys we were adding still another project to our overloaded schedule. We were starting regular classes, open to all comers, in nutrition, hygiene and such matters. There was entirely too much disease caused by ignorance in "our town." We might as well get after it right now.

Every day from dawn to high noon, we held sick call at the hospital. In the afternoon we loaded our faithful jeep and held "jeep call" in the surrounding countryside. Often Pete and Denny were in charge when I had surgery to do. Then, in the evenings, the crowd would gather in front of our house for Walt Disney movies and for our lectures on the facts of living, delivered via our proud interpreter, Chai.

Chai was so proud of his job as interpreter for the Americans that he even bought himself a pair of shoes while on a visit to Vientiane so as to live up to his station. But he walked with such a painful gait that it lasted only a few days; then he was barefoot again on the soft sod of Laos. He only put those shoes on for very special occasions after that.

Sick call was always an ordeal for, in addition to disease and ignorance, we had to contend with the quaint customs of the people. The line would sometimes form double in the crowded courtyard and file into the dispensary. I would sit in a chair, with Chai beside me, and try to get the patient to sit on the bench facing me. That wasn't as easy as it sounds.

To the people of Vang Vieng, the American doctor was a "mandarin"—high on the social totem pole. The trouble was that, according to established custom, the humble Laotian's head must never be higher than the mandarin's. As a result, when examining a patient, I had to bend or squat lower and lower. Sometimes I had to grovel on the dirty floor in order to listen to a heartbeat!

We also had our troubles with the Lao nurses we were trying to train. These earnest, intelligent boys and girls would perform any duty, no matter how unpleasant it might be. But at first we could not get them to clean a head wound or even hold a patient's head while I stitched the scalp or pulled a tooth. This was because the people of Laos believed that the spirit of Buddha resides in the head, so that even touching it is to defile the tabernacle.

Obstetrics was our biggest problem from the outset. About fifty per cent of the babies were lost before or during childbirth and one out of every five mothers died. For this reason we gave high priority to our program for training midwives. When we arrived in Vang Vieng, there were about four practicing midwives and perhaps as many more young girls who wanted to learn the calling. We won them over to our side, had them help around the hospital, and made them promise to call us for each childbirth. When we went on a call, we would always take along one or two of the younger girls. And, always, we carried a bag containing the wonderful midwife's kit which had been given us by CARE.

After each girl had served her apprenticeship, and had herself delivered twenty-five babies under our watchful eyes, we gave her one of the CARE kits—always the one I had personally carried. So, just as in America nurses are "capped" at graduation, we "bagged" our midwives at Vang Vieng.

Nor was our medical practice only confined to humans. One day a man came to Pete and explained the symptoms from which a "friend" of his was suffering. This friend lacked pep, was unable to hold his head up, had bad feet, and was losing weight. The man said that all these things had come upon his friend a few weeks after he had been mauled by a tiger. "How old is your friend?" Pete asked. The man had no idea. Peter asked many more questions and finally said that the man would have to bring his friend to the clinic.

The man said he had done this already; his friend was tied up outside the hospital. Peter went outside and found the friend, a small Tibetan pony, tethered to a tree. Pete called to me and I joined the consultation. The pony was in bad shape. The tiger had torn his throat and chest and had slashed open his forehead. Each claw mark was infested with maggots. I sent for soap, water and cotton and proceeded to wash and clean the sores. Pete injected quantities of penicillin. Each day this patient came back to us looking a little better. At last we were able to discharge him from the active treatment list.

It was now too late to save ourselves. The word spread, and hardly a week passed that someone did not bring a horse or a water buffalo to us for treatment. The animals had as many complaints as the two-legged patients: bad eyes, coughs, loss of weight, fever, or just old age.

After we had been in Laos a few weeks, a twenty-year-old boy named "Si" joined our team. He became our housekeeper, cook, bottlewasher and handyman. Si had the features of an eleven-year-old boy and he took great pride in his two gold teeth, a mark of wealth in this neck of the woods. Si took loving, tender care of his Americans. Having a coolie, a cook, a houseboy, an interpreter and other servants in Laos is a different thing than it is in America. These people were not "employees" to us, they were members of our team. They ate with us, bathed with us, swam with us, worked with us, and came out on night calls with us. Later they became very devoted to us and we, in our turn, grew to love them all very much.

Our domestic life was very monotonous. It was the

same every day—long lines at the hospital, worrisome diseases, stink and misery. The food we ate was also monotonous. As we did not wish to catch dysentery, we decided to be very cautious. The Navy had given us a large supply of C-rations to help us in our dietary problems. Aside from the first day, when sheer agony forced us to eat Chinese soup, we lived on C-rations for many, many months. Pete, whose job it was to supervise the cooking, was a man of imagination. Without any chef's training whatsoever, Peter was able to concoct a masterpiece for each meal. Our only complaint was that it was always the same masterpiece!

C-rations come in dull green and grey cans that make you feel bilious just to look at them. The food consists of: can one, beans and meat; can two, beef stew; can three, pork sausage without gravy; can four, beef and peas; can five, chicken and noodles. Peter would change off between these five choices and mix the food with locally cooked rice, skilfully blending into this mess just the right amount of B-1. What is B-1? This is another C-ration nightmare consisting of crackers, cocoa and jam. So that we could have breaded rice and meat, Peter cooked this glorious mixture together. Port Arthur, Texas' gift to Dr. Dooley was Peter Sherrer Kessey and his culinary masterpieces!

It was easy enough to joke about our food and very necessary to do so. For when you are living in a jungle on the edge of the world, small things have a way of looming large. If you are not careful they will overwhelm you. In order to keep our mental balance, it was very important for us to hold on to our sense of humor.

As the weeks passed, we became more and more famous. We always urged the villagers to pay us in barter for our medicine and for our treatments. This was important for the sake of their own pride and it was important for us too. It was costing a lot to run this mission. I had made all my plans for northern Laos and most of the equipment I had bought was geared to cold weather. But because we had not been allowed to go to the north, we needed a lot of different equipment. And I had to buy it. Therefore I was constantly worried that my money would run out before I could get to my original destination, the north of Laos. Any saving of money was important to us and the simple idea of having our patients pay us in produce made a big difference. At the end of a day in the clinic we might have a dozen eggs, several coconuts, perhaps a bottle of the local whiskey and, if the day was good, a scrawny chicken.

The sick call that we held every morning at our hospital was pretty routine. But the afternoon "jeep calls" were full of surprises. A jeep call meant that two members of our team would drive to one of the dozens of outlying villages around Vang Vieng. The jeep would come into the village with its horn blaring. We would park, drop the tail gate, send someone for a bucket of water, and open the boxes of medicines. At once our portable clinic would be the focus of a thriving practice. The people who came to us in the afternoons were those who were either too sick or not sick enough to make it to Vang Vieng which was about a four hour walk away.

The crowding that was part of our clinic work was absent at jeep call. We had fresh air and we could move around. We knew that it was important to go into the huts of these people. They had never seen an American before! They had never welcomed white men into their homes, and they are just as proud of their homes as we are. I think we must have been in over three thousand of these Asian homes. Inside those huts it was often hot and humid. By our standards most of them were filthy, and they swarmed with lice, fleas, gnats and other insects. Always in the darkest corners were the pot-bellied children, the undernourished, the malnourished, and the miserable.

We always carried a black bag, a must for M.D.'s in America and a good idea in Laos, too. We kept the jeep well stocked with antibiotics, "Meals for Millions," sterile solutions, T-shirts and perhaps some candy to bribe the young and old. A stateside friend sent me a boxful of small American flags. We had one huge flag flying over our house and we kept others tacked to medical bags, kits and boxes. Denny managed to fasten one little flag on the fender of our jeep. It was often torn by the brambles along the jungle trail and spattered by mud, but nevertheless it served proudly as our symbol of home.

We did not bleat about the glories of stateside plumbing; we didn't say a word about Mount Vernon; we didn't praise the democratic system; we didn't try to convert anyone to anything. We wanted to be associated with only two things: the first was the American flag; the second was the phrase with which we had our interpreter begin every statement, *"Thank mo America pun va . . . the American doctor says."* We believed in deeds and not in words.

It was wonderful work and I had wonderful helpers. I can't give enough praise to the three men who were with me and the two boys who joined up later. These men did the dirty work, seldom grumbling and usually joking a bit. They were excellent men in every sense of the word. Peter Kessey had a willing heart and a gentle hand; he spoke to the people in a Texas-American accent, and somehow they always seemed to understand him. Norman Baker, my French-speaking mechanic and general man around the place, could slap on a dressing that was guaranteed never to come off; he would sweat and grunt but he got it on and it stayed on. Denny Shepard, who was going on to medical school, was brilliant and practiced a high grade of medicine. I am afraid Dooley was a hard task-master. I often lost my temper, but the boys persisted. I believe that my men showed heroism, sacrifice and guts, not in any one great dramatic action, but steadily, day after day.

Later on, when my new recruits from the University of Notre Dame had joined me and we said the family rosary aloud at night, I heard Protestant Pete Kessey complaining about it. "Seems you can hardly get to sleep at night, up there in the jungle, what with their clicking their beads all the time."

But I know that those prayers were the biggest help of all.

CHAPTER TEN

"Phasing Out"

One day in November we were busy as usual. At midday we just bolted our food and went back to work. Nobody mentioned it but all of us were aware of the fact that this was Thanksgiving Day. We were just a little more homesick than usual. Then along toward dusk we heard the roar of a jeep. A cloud of dust boiled up the road to our house and out stepped Jeff Cheek of Comanche, Texas. Jeff, who was attached to the USOM in Vientiane, was one of our few visitors and he couldn't come often. As soon as he got out of his jeep he demanded to know what we had to eat.

"C-rations, brother!" Pete said. "Today it's beef and peas plus rice." Jeff laughed and produced a dusty bag out of the back of his jeep. It held a complete Thanksgiving dinner: roast turkey, cranberry sauce, mashed potatoes, pumpkin pie.

It was a wonderful surprise. Life in the jungle isn't easy. I personally lived to a certain extent in a state of fear all the time I was in Laos. Fear of isolation, fear of loneliness and fear of the great forest that was all around us.

That Thanksgiving Day feast is something I will never forget. After we had gorged ourselves, we sat on the porch and talked about a little girl called Savong whom Jeff had brought with him the very first time he came to see us.

Jeff had been driving along the jungle trail, when a group of natives stopped his jeep and asked for help. They showed him a girl, about fourteen years old, lying on a mat. She was only half conscious and Jeff could see she was near to death.

This was Savong. Some time earlier, no one knew how long ago, she had scratched her leg in the jungle and it had become infected. Savong's people didn't know what to do, so they just left her lying in the hut. In time, the entire leg became horribly bloated and the infection spread up into the groin. That was the way Jeff found her.

He put her in the back of his jeep, and drove slowly through the jungle, reaching Vang Vieng after dark. We opened up the hospital but after one look I had my doubts about saving her. But there was something about Savong that touched us deeply. In her we saw all the miserable, neglected kids in Laos. Southeast Asia is full of Savongs. So we were determined to save her.

Of course she was terribly dirty after such long neglect and before we could go any further, we had to scrub her nearly lifeless little body with soap and brush. Then we gave her as little anesthesia as possible and began to operate. When we got through there was nothing left of that big, bloated leg but bone and a few soggy muscles.

Pete, Denny, Baker and even Chai took turns watching over Savong all through that night and the next day.

The fever dropped, she brightened, and then she began to cry. Not from pain now, but because her torture was over. Between sobs we heard her mumbling *"Cop chai, cop chai, cop chai"* over and over: "Thank you, thank you, thank you."

Weeks passed and Savong grew stronger. First she sat up, then she walked a few steps. The boys trimmed her hair in a sort of feather bob, gave her a toothbrush and taught her how to use it. Somehow they even got some girls' clothes for her. Then Jeff came with presents of hair ribbons and combs. We decided that Savong really looked beautiful.

Months later we discharged her. She was strong and well, although she limped a bit on that frail leg. Her people came and took her back to her home. Before she left we took a picture of her. Whenever we felt especially homesick or disheartened we would look at that picture of Savong. It served to remind us that, for some people, things might have been different had we stayed comfortably at home.

Our classes in sanitation, hygiene, food and nutrition, infant and child care, were paying off handsomely. We had "bagged" many midwives and these girls were dedicated to their work. They had made "midwifery" into such a proud profession that it attracted other candidates. The Lao nurses were increasing in both number and skill. Each fortnight when the boys drove into Vientiane for mail and supplies, they would bring back a senior from the *lycée* to stay with us a week. We hoped that in this way these young men would be inspired to study medicine. Already we had trained a dozen "practical nurses," more than were really needed in Vang Vieng.

I knew that the time had come when we must "phase out" of Vang Vieng. My mission, as I saw it, was not to set up a permanent American outpost. I just wanted to begin something that the Laos themselves would be able to take over and continue. True, it would be primitive by western standards; but it would be much better than what these people had had before. And it would belong to them.

It is my belief that if you want to help people in a foreign land, you must be content to begin like that. There were Americans in Vientiane who said that I practiced nineteenth century medicine. They were correct. And when I left, our native personnel would practice eighteenth century medicine. Since most of the villagers are living in the fifteenth century, I call this progress.

Part of the plan was already settled in my mind. Kam Lak, the senior nurse, would take charge. He was a devoted, highly intelligent young man who could already be trusted with minor surgery. His wife, who was probably our best midwife, could serve as his assistant. We would leave them a few surgical instruments and about $1,000 worth of drugs. The Ministry promised them more supplies.

My boys had stayed with me as long as they had promised. Within the next month they would have to leave for home. Baker was anxious to get back to his wife and baby; Denny Shepard, who also had a bride waiting, had to get back to the University, as did Pete Kessey. I had two replacements lined up; I was just waiting for one more letter from South Bend, Indiana, to clinch the deal.

I decided it was time for me to make a trip to Vientiane

and get everything arranged. On January 2nd, 1957 we arrived in the capital. I went directly to see Dr. Oudom at the Ministry of Health. He greeted me with enthusiasm and told me that the Premier wanted to see me. We went right over to the Ministry and, after a short wait, were ushered into the Premier's office.

The Premier spoke glowingly of my mission in Vang Vieng. To my surprise he seemed to know every detail of our work there. He knew about the nurse and midwife training programs, the hygiene and sanitation classes, the jeep call system, etc. Then he asked me about my plans for the future.

I told him that my funds were running low and that I could only stay in Laos about four more months. This was because it was Dooley, and not rich old Uncle Sam, who was footing the bills!

It was then that he made me his fine offer. Beginning at once, he said, the Royal Lao Government would provide "all the facilities" for our work. This meant that the army would furnish transport and supplies. The Ministry of Education would give me anything I needed for an educational program. I would have free access to the government's medical supplies. The government would even pay the salaries of my Lao personnel. This was astonishing news.

It was almost too good to be true. But I decided I might as well shoot for the moon. "Your Excellency," I said, "don't you think my medical mission could do more for the Royal Government if you sent me into one of the northern provinces?"

"I most certainly do!" he said. I looked over and saw Dr. Oudom's beaming smile.

There were two possible areas of operation, the Premier said, Muong Sing, a town near the Burma-China border and—Nam Tha!

My original goal! I was so elated by this good news that I found it hard to concentrate on what the Premier was telling me. Both Muong Sing and Nam Tha, he explained, had operational landing strips now. He would put a small plane at my disposal and he would keep a supply line open. Of course there were still dangers in the north, but there were police and soldiers who would act as my bodyguard.

When I told Ambassador Parsons at the American Embassy my good news, he seemed delighted. "I think it's a fine idea for you to go up north now, Dr. Dooley," he said. "Conditions in Laos are more stable now and the air strip at Nam Tha makes it possible for us to keep in touch with you."

Now all that was left for me to do was to "close out" at Vang Vieng. I told the boys my good news and they listened to me with mixed feelings.

Baker had already booked his passage home, but Denny decided to go up to Nam Tha with me for a few weeks and help me get settled. And Peter Kessey, the lone bachelor of the trio, made an even bigger sacrifice.

"Well shucks," he said, "they can get along without me at pharmacy school. I'll string along with you for a few more months, Doc."

In Vang Vieng we told Chai and Si of the new plan and that of course we wanted them to go along. They moaned a little at first but then they decided to come with us. "Where you go, we will come always."

We did not want to offend the village by leaving too suddenly, so we decided to spend four or five weeks doing our work as usual. Each day at sick call we explained that we must leave but that the Lao nurse and midwives would carry on. We also promised to leave the "miracle medicines" of the white man for the villagers.

To say goodbye, the town of Vang Vieng gave us a *baci,* a sort of ritual ceremony climaxed by a feast. The women of the village built a small pyramid of palm leaves and decorated it with flowers, candles and baubles. It was then placed in a bowl and hung with cotton streamers. Around the base of this edifice the women arranged tasty morsels of pork, rice, sweetmeats and other delicacies.

Then we all sat in a circle on mats, close enough to the center pyramid to be able to lean forward and touch the bowl with outstretched hands.

An old sorcerer now began to chant the Invocation to the Spirits. He asked Sakke, who lives in the Paradise of Sixteen Floors, to come and join us. He begged Khirisi, who dwells in the mountains to come with Attarikhe who abounds in Sweet Air. The old sorcerer didn't forget to invite a single Spirit to come to the *baci.*

Then he addressed the souls of those for whom the *baci* was given. The Lao tribes feel that the soul is a vagabond, and must be recalled to the body from time to time. "Come, be with us, Souls," he chanted, "return to your home of flesh." As the Laos think that there are thirty-two parts to the human body and that each of them has a soul, this incantation took a long time. When both the spirits and the souls had finally arrived, we could sit back and rest a moment.

Now the second part of the *baci* began. The sorcerer took a piece of cotton string from the center pyramid and knelt in front of me. He made a wish for me and, while chanting this wish, tied a string around my wrist, carefully twirling the ends so that the wish could not fall out of the string. Then a second person tied another string on my wrist, and a third, and so on. Each of us, for whom the *baci* was given, got the same treatment. By the time the ceremony was over, we had more than a dozen cotton strings apiece around our wrists. And with each string came a wish:

"May you be strong against the tusks of elephants."

"May you be rich."

"May you have many wives."

"May your jeep not fall off the road nor your airplane from the sky."

"May you return to us your friends."

Chai had coached us. Upon receiving the *baci*, the honored person must do his part to show his gratitude. So after each string was tied, we clasped our hands together as if we praying and said, "*Chop chai liiiiii, saaaa.*"

When the *baci* was at last finished, the sorcerer thanked the spirits and the souls and we all ate the food that the spirits hadn't eaten.

At last the day came when we had to leave. We sat on the front porch of our empty house, waiting for the army trucks that the Minister was sending to get us.

Hundreds of villagers had gathered in the square to say goodbye to us. The *baci* strings they had tied around our "wrists" reached almost to our elbows. The people of Vang Vieng brought many going-away gifts: flowers, corn, chicken, the local whiskey. Again and again we said goodbye to everybody from the mayor to the kids. We were all sitting around feeling sad; but we consoled ourselves with the thought that the trucks would soon arrive and we could then work off our melancholy in the sweat of loading.

We waited all morning; we waited all afternoon. We unrolled our sleeping bags and slept all night. Next day the trucks arrived. The army drivers did not explain the delay. Nor did we ask for an explanation. By now we had grown used to this sort of thing; it no longer bothered us.

Our last glimpse of the villagers of Vang Vieng touched us. As we jolted along toward the jungle road, we saw them waving with all their hearts. But they were waving their arms *towards* themselves in the parting gesture of Laos that means "come back soon."

CHAPTER ELEVEN

Nam Tha at Last

When we reached Vientiane, there was the usual mix-up. Norman Baker, who was returning to his wife and family, barely made his plane because of a last-minute change in schedule. He just managed to get aboard before the plane door closed. As they took off, I suddenly realized that my friend Norman Baker had left and that I hadn't had time to thank him for all he had done.

While Denny stayed in Vientiane to make preparations for the move to Nam Tha, Pete and I flew to Bangkok to meet our two new volunteers. Their names were John de Vitry and Robert E. Waters; both of them were undergraduates at Notre Dame, my own alma mater.

We saw them get off the plane at the Bangkok airport, two typical crewcut college boys, somewhat the worse for wear after their forty-five-hour flight. Pete groaned, "O Lord, Joe College and his roommate. I'll bet they've even brought their hi-fi gear and record albums!"

John de Vitry was a tall, slim, sensitive and serious-minded fellow, twenty-one years old. Bob Waters was only twenty, but tall, well built and obviously an extrovert. They both looked pretty soft and green for the part of the world where we were going to operate.

92

But both boys turned out to be prodigious workers. John was a diplomat, something the Dooley mission needed badly. Within thirty days they were both crusty and uncomplaining veterans taking life on the China border in their stride. I guess we all have to start somewhere.

We left Vientiane in a huge, old Bristol cargo plane that had a belly like a landing craft, tremendous wings and a pair of undersized propellers. For the next three hours we flew north over a cloud layer pierced now and then by jagged mountain peaks. Then we descended and saw the vast rain forest of the Nam Tha valley.

The French pilot made several passes at the little landing strip and began to climb again. *"Trop petite!"* he said. The muddy strip was too short for the big Bristol. I went to the cockpit to persuade the pilot to try again. He looked at me pityingly and shrugged his shoulders. Then he swooped in and skidded to a stop. There were only a few feet of runway to spare.

A big crowd was on hand to meet us. We opened the plane doors and jumped down to the ground. At last we had arrived on the soil of the north! We were in the northernmost fingertip of freedom jammed into the underbelly of Communist China. None of us said very much. We knew that halfway up that first range of hills just north of us was the rim of hell.

Nam Tha was a bigger and more progressive village than Vang Vieng. It had a public "square" lined with houses and shops, an elaborate Buddhist temple, a police headquarters, a jail and the "mansion" of the Governor of the Province.

The house we were to live in was solidly built. It was

big but we weren't going to have it all to ourselves. We had to share it with a telegraph office, the operator and his large family, and a couple of young school teachers. We asked everyone to stay in the quarters they already had. Then we divided the rest of the house amongst ourselves. Chai, Si and Kieu, our new interpreter, had one room; Bob, Denny and I shared two large rooms; and Pete, who loved his privacy, inhabited a small, dark closet which he named "The Black Hole."

Only a short walk from the house was the dispensary building which had been completed only recently. As soon as we could, we began work on the hospital. We made the main dispensary building into the main hospital. It was about thirty-five feet long, divided into three rooms. One room we left in the hands of the Lao nurses, the second we used as an office and the third became the sick call room. We built a large table, covered it with linoleum and put it in the sick call room. At the house we had a small generator that we used for the movie projector. In Vientiane we had bought a bright desk lamp; we hooked this to the table and on to the generator. Now we had an operating room.

Next to the Clinic was an abandoned bamboo building. We cleaned this up, painted it, built fifteen beds out of teak wood and old army cots, pasted some old pictures we had cut out of magazines on to the walls to brighten up the place. It looked fine by anyone's standards. Now we were ready for business.

We even had a sort of "isolation ward" for leprosy cases, a small, thatched hut, big enough to hold nine cots. So, before long, we had a three-building hospital!

Denny decided to spend the short time he would still

be with us setting up an efficient surgery. He went to work installing equipment, sterilizing instruments, and making sterile packs. It was a good thing he did, for surgery started sooner than we expected.

On our second day in Nam Tha we heard a great commotion. Escorted by the Governor himself, some natives appeared at our compound carrying two "sedan chairs," crudely made out of bamboo and slung on poles. I went out, had a look at the occupants and yelled to the boys to get the operating room ready for an emergency.

It seems that some bandits had swooped down on this Lao tribesman's hut in a little border village. They had hacked at the occupants with long swords, literally quartering the grandmother and a small child and wounding the tribesman and his wife. The neighbors, hearing screams, came running to the hut. But the bandits had fled. They stole nothing.

The villagers put the wounded victims in the "sling chairs" and brought them to Nam Tha. It was a gruelling journey that took a day and a night and I will never know how that poor couple survived.

The woman's head, face and breasts had been slashed to ribbons. The husband's scalp had been lifted from the skull by one sweep of a sharp sword. His jaw bone was broken in several places and one side of his face was slashed away from the eyelid down to the lip.

We operated, filled them up with antibiotics, antitetanus shots, intravenous feeding, and spent hours suturing their gashed bodies. They pulled through.

The Governor and one of his officers stayed in the operating room until the whole bloody operation was over. Then the Governor went outside and lit a cigarette.

After I had washed up, I went outside, and found him there.

"That's the way it goes," he said. "We'll send out a patrol and find nothing. For a while that village can sleep in peace. Then the devils will strike somewhere else."

This was Communism. It was much in evidence in Nam Tha and I began to understand why Ambassador Parsons had not wanted us to work in this area.

The next night we were busy with another "basket case." This time it wasn't Communism: it was witch doctors.

Toward nightfall a man came to our house and begged us to save his ten year old son who lay near death in the mountain village of Ban Pereng. What was wrong? The boy had been burned, the man said, "black like a pig." When had this happened?

"Fourteen nights ago," the man said. "The night was very cold. Ion, my son, wore three extra shirts to keep warm. He backed so close to the fire that his shirt burst into flames."

The soldier who had brought us the man, told us to wait till morning. He said the trail to Ban Pareng was treacherous even when used in broad daylight. But the father was frantic. The case sounded serious and besides, we would be busy in the morning with sick call. So Pete, Denny and Chai found flashlights, and I checked the contents of my bag. Then we told the man to lead the way.

Now we learned why it was no use having a jeep in Nam Tha. Walking in single file, we made our way through the jungle. Then we found the mountain trail and started to climb. For the next couple of hours we clambered up steep rocks and crossed rope-and-bamboo bridges that swayed dangerously over rivers that were like rushing torrents. An old man of thirty, I was exhausted when we finally reached the little village of Ban Pereng.

We were taken to a large, gloomy hut, perched high on stilts. The room reeked with the smell of burnt flesh. The father led us to what looked like a pile of rags lying in one corner. In the light of my flash I saw a boy sprawled flat on his stomach.

He was charred black from shoulders to buttocks. Barely conscious, he lay without moving in the most distorted position. Yet the boy's whole back seemed to be in motion. I pushed the light closer. The back was swarming with maggots that were feasting on the charred flesh.

The father told me that after the accident a witch doctor had come. He had smeared the burns with a paste which I later learned was made of pig grease, betel nut juice and cow dung. The deep third degree burns were bad enough. But this crazy treatment, probably repeated several times during the past fortnight, had helped to produce this horrible living death.

There was nothing we could do then and there. If the boy stayed in that hut much longer, he would certainly die. But getting him down that mountain and into Nam Tha seemed almost impossible. Yet that was our only chance. We told the father to find a large basket, some rope and a strong pole. Pete and Chai stayed behind to direct the "ambulance" operation. Denny and I found a guide and started back to Nam Tha.

We were scrubbed up and ready when our basket

case arrived at the hospital some hours later. We put Ion on the table and went to work. It was much worse than I had expected. But at last Ion was bundled in fluff gauze and antiseptic ointment and was carried gently to a bed. After weeks of neglect, with little food or water, he was weak and dehydrated. When we tried to give him fluids intravenously, we couldn't find a vein that hadn't collapsed. That boy was so thin we even had trouble finding muscles that would take a penicillin injection.

Denny and Pete spent what was left of the night pushing fluids subcutaneously into Ion's body. The children of Laos are used to hardship and pain. And Ion had the guts he needed. With the power of medicine, blended with the power of prayer, and sprinkled with a little sweat, he pulled through. When he woke he found his bed decorated with colored balloons and he found his day and night corpsmen very happy.

I learned something from that night. All my boys wanted the job of sitting up with Ion. These young men elected to devote their weariest hours to that child because we live in one world. The brotherhood of man does exist, as surely as does the Fatherhood of God. In the end, all of us are our brothers' keepers.

Before we came to Nam Tha, the witch doctors had ruled supreme. No one ever questioned their wisdom or their power to cure. But now the poor people had seen the American doctor. And they were torn between the magic of the sorcerers they had always known and the new ways of the white medicine men.

Finally the witch doctors put a "hex" on our hospital. They placed little mats of woven bamboo on short posts stuck in the ground all around our compound. And for a while no one, no matter how ill he might be, would come near our hospital for help.

All the witch doctors were respected village elders. But our two most powerful adversaries were Old Joe and a crone we called "Maggie."

At last we decided to adopt the old American stratagem: "If you can't lick 'em, join 'em." We began to treat the witch doctors like "colleagues in the healing arts." Our attitude was that they just happened to practice a type of medicine that was different from ours; we disagreed with them and yet we respected them.

One afternoon I came back from an emergency call in the jungle to find Pete having an earnest professional talk with Old Joe. Pete gave me the eye and I squatted down and listened respectfully.

Old Joe had spread out in front of him a weird assortment of sticks, bamboo slivers, betel nuts, boiled leaves, pig grease and cow dung. He was explaining the theory behind his collection of "drugs." Most of it was fantastic. But every now and then I recognized the echo of old folk remedies (like the use of spider webs in open wounds) which even modern medicine considers effective.

"Well," said Pete, "we just belong to different schools of medicine. We use different drugs, different methods, but both of us are working for the same thing. We both want to cure people of disease and suffering. The important thing is for us to work together. We'll teach you what we know and you will teach us what you know." That sounded fair enough to Old Joe.

From that day on Old Joe rarely missed a sick call. We would give a shot of penicillin, Joe would invoke the proper spirits. We would splint a fracture, then allow

Old Joe to tie his red, white and black strings around the splints. If we were paid two coconuts as a fee, Old Joe got one. And, because his recovery rate had never been so high before, Old Joe was happy. He became our staunch friend.

Maggie was my own special problem. She was a snaggle-toothed old crone, and the dirtiest woman in the whole village. She dressed in a ragged, western-style blouse and skirt with a filthy towel wrapped around her head. Maggie shaved her head regularly, but she never washed her hands.

After handling each patient, I would carefully wash my hands in soap and water, then hold them out while an assistant poured alcohol over them. Maggie, who rarely left my side during sick call, watched this procedure in a fascinated way. I explained to her that soap and water plus some of the strong liquid had the power to banish any "evil spirits" that might be clinging to my hand from a dirty wound. Maggie nodded knowingly. Explained in this way the germ theory made good sense to her.

One day a small child came to us with a head covered with sores. I handed Maggie a bottle of strong shampoo and told her to take the child to the river and give him a good scrub. When she came back the child's scalp was bleeding in places, but it was clean! During the washing process, Maggie's own hands had become cleaner than they had been in years. But that wasn't enough for Maggie! She went to Chai and held out her cupped hands. He poured alcohol over them and she "scrubbed up." Maggie was learning!

And the witch doctors were not the only ones who were

beginning to learn about the white men's medicine. In Nam Tha we could not teach elementary hygiene and sanitation in formal classes as we had done in Vang Vieng, because there were so many people in this village that we had to give all our time to treating the sick and injured. So we decided to hold sick call in such a way that each case became a demonstration. When a child was placed before us with this or that illness, we would teach the mother not only how she must take care of this particular sickness, but also how she could prevent it from coming back another time. The whole crowd that was sitting in front of the open doors on the porch, would listen to what we were saying. They were eager to learn. They did not enjoy being miserable any more than you or I would; they wanted to be healthier and they understood perfectly that they did not always have to be sick.

Often we lectured to people, taking a homemade blackboard with us and talking to a whole village. But what worked much better was to take a sick little child, show it to everybody in the clinic, and from this living example explain what could be done in the way of cure and prevention. And we had over a hundred of these pathetic cases every single day!

Once a tribesman came to us all the way from the western China-Burma frontier. He had a wound on his foot that had been neglected so long that most of his foot was now one gaping hole. We asked him how many days it took to travel to us. "A great many," he said. He then told us that our work was known even that far up in the western hills. We slept well that night: evidently our candle was giving a good light.

CHAPTER TWELVE

The Great Float

The "Great Float" was John de Vitry's idea. As it was almost impossible to travel in jungle country, he suggested that we float down the Nam Tha River in small boats, holding sick call in all the lonely villages along the way.

At first the Governor was violently against the scheme. He argued that the river was treacherous, even impassable in places, and that the people who lived in those isolated villages were hostile to white men. Most of the political prisoners in his stockade, he added, had come from this region. Even his soldiers did not dare to venture more than a few miles down the river for mopping-up operations. In any case, he doubted that we could find boatmen who would be willing to risk their necks on that kind of a trip.

I sent a message to Dr. Oudom in Vietiane, and he promptly sent us back his approval. The old Governor threw up his hands and said *he* would not be responsible for us. But nevertheless he not only insisted on sending a party of armed guards in advance of us, but even assigned four gun-toting soldiers to go along with our party.

We planned to travel in *pirogues*, the Lao version of the dugout canoe. These were the only boats able to shoot the rapids. The Governor was right about one thing: we had plenty of trouble signing up the boatmen. No one had made the whole trip from Nam Tha to the Mekong. And in addition to the rapids and the bandits who were said to be at large, there would be the heavy monsoon rains. However, extra pay reinforced by some persuasion by the Governor did the trick.

John lined up three *pirogues*, each with a crew of four men. Two men sat in the middle of the dugout and paddled, the others mounted the "flying platform" fore and aft and used the long oars that did the steering. We divided our medical supplies, food, and camping equipment among the three boats, so that if one was lost we would still be able to eat, sleep and hold sick call.

We were scheduled to leave at dawn, but following the usual Lao pattern, we heaved anchor only a little before lunchtime. We were ready to go bright and early and were down at the *pirogues* with all our equipment. The chief boatman was to come down in just a few minutes. But it was a good hour before he came ambling toward us. He took a look around, then said that he would have to go back to the Governor to get a paper of some sort. The interpreter told us he was afraid the boatmen were getting cold feet. They were worried about the bandits and the treacherous river and they demanded more money for such a trip. It was a holdup, but I can't say I blamed them.

At last they returned from the Governor's. We said

goodbye again to the dozens friends who had come to see us off. It had begun to drizzle, so I squatted inside the little bamboo hut that was in the middle of the long dugout. When the boatman got aboard I yelled, "Heave anchor!" in good Navy style . . . but we did not heave anchor. The chief boatman did not like the way his assistants—and the Americans—had loaded the cargo.

We had to unpack and rearrange all the gear in accordance with the boatman's orders concerning weight, and my own orders concerning value of equipment. At long last we seemed to be loaded properly and without any more goodbyes, we sort of drifted away from shore. By this time it was raining torrents. It did not stop for the next four days.

The first afternoon's "float," as we blithely referred to rapid shooting, was as scary as it was interesting. One boatman stood on the bow of the slender dugout and one on the stern, each armed with a huge paddle for steering. Two other men squatted just inboard of them with short oars, used for thrusting along. They did not have to stroke very much because the Nam Tha River current took care of that, shooting us along with alternating heaves.

The boatmen wove a palm leaf covering under which we sat, hunched over on the wet floor of the canoe. But it did not take long for the rain to break through the leaves; after which we were just as wet inside as we were out.

Our first stop was about three hours down the river. The boatmen got out and waded into the jungle to hack down some large green bamboo logs to attach to the side of the boat. This was because we were rocking so badly, and the rapids were worse than he had expected. The river here had no bank. The monsoon-flooded waters had risen so high here that there were large bushes and trees smack in the middle of the river, and the edges were not banks at all but simply trees on which the water had climbed up several feet. When we came to our first big rapid, the *pirogues* pulled over to the side again.

This time we had to get out, carrying the most valuable equipment, and plunge through the deep jungle on foot. We walked along the side of the river while the boats shot the rough part of the rapid, bouncing off rocks, slithering between logs and racing over the wild, white foam. Suddenly they came out into a small, quiet whirlpool and were able to paddle over to the edge where we were standing, knee-deep in water, with camera and gear over our heads, as the rain poured down on them. And so passed our first day, stopping, diving along the edge of the rapid, getting back aboard again. All this in the midst of that constant, drenching, chilly monsoon rain.

That first night we reached a small village where only a few women could be found. With our four gun-toting guards we looked more like an invasion force than a medical mission. The frightened women told us that their men had gone hunting in the jungle but would be back later. They took us to the village guest house, which was a depressing place. We managed, somehow, to wash up and dry ourselves around a fire. Then we heated up some C-rations, set up the mosquito nets, unrolled the bedding and went to sleep, dreaming of good food and hard, dry land.

When I woke the next morning, the whole village was

milling around our hut. We weren't frightened of the crowd because we knew that we were still so near to Nam Tha that many of our visitors must have come to our hospital. Sure enough, we soon recognized some of our old patients. There were not many people there in need of attention, because they often came on to Nam Tha.

Although the weather was as bad as ever, the trip that day was ten times more interesting. We plunged down into deep gorges, but instead of Colorado River-like cliffs on each side, we were hedged in by huge trees. I was constantly yelling to the boys in the other boat, and they were calling back to me: "Look at that animal!" "Did you see that—was it a bird? Was it a monkey?"

We stopped at several villages that day and at one we ate our C-ration lunch. Each village seemed to have its own private epidemic. Because there was no trading up and down that river, the various diseases did not spread. In some villages there was whooping cough, in others dysentery. Everywhere there were scabies, ringworm, beriberi, malaria, worms and yaws.

We spent our second night at a poor village that was terribly isolated—even from Nam Tha. As we walked up the side of the jungle into the cleared area where the village stood clinging to the mountain slope, we asked for the house of the chieftain. When we got the directions, we walked ahead, all the villagers trailing along behind us. Suddenly a man stepped out of the crowd leading his small son. He fell on his knees before us, clasped his hands before his face and thanked us because we had cured the boy. The child walked up to John and threw his arms around him. He had been one of our first cases. Seeing that the little boy had no fear, for he had known the tenderness and compassion of my assistants, the rest of the villagers accepted us. Then the chieftain came to the top of his stairs and beckoned to us to enter his house.

This chieftain was a grand old fellow. We asked him if he had ever seen white men before. "No." We asked him if he or his family, who were sitting around, thought that we were funny looking. His truthful answer was "Yes."

The whole village found us Americans fascinating. They enjoyed watching us open our cans, cook dinner and eat with our bizarre instruments. To these villagers we were the greatest show on earth. But our "miracle medicines" were most welcome. Here, many of the villagers seemed to have something wrong with them, but I didn't see any psychosomatic diseases. And during my whole year in Laos I never came across a single case of neurosis.

According to the old map, the halfway point for us would be the village of Nale. Nale was pretty much like the other villages, except that it was a little bigger and had a police outpost. It was raining, of course, when the village chief came out to welcome us. This man had spent several years in Vientiane during the French occupation, so he could not only read and write, he could even speak French!

We held a long sick call here. It lasted well into the night. We treated a woman with a tumor, a boy with a type of eye ailment that turns the eyeball into a whitish, protruding globe, several cases of hernia, and other minor diseases.

The village chieftain threw a party for us and then took us to the guest house. Because the guards the Governor had sent ahead of us had told him we were coming, he had had some beds built for the white men. "You know those odd white men do not sleep on stuffed leaf mats on the floor like normal people do. For some peculiar reason they like to put their mattresses on a wooden frame and call it a bed!" (Why do we?) In any case he had had the beds built for us but the measurements were a little off. If you lay perfectly still they were just wide enough to lie either on your back or your stomach. If you tried to roll over, you would roll off for sure. Poor six-foot Bob really had a dangerous night.

Early the next day we were off again. Several hours later another *pirogue* caught up with us. There was a frantic father in this boat who lived north of Nale. The night before, his sister had seen us and had discovered that we were the white doctors from Nam Tha. She had set off at once by foot to her brother's village and had returned with him this morning. They had brought his dying daughter to see us but we had already left the village. So they had borrowed a boat and had come down to catch us.

We could not land anywhere because of the river and the jungle. He shot down on the rapids with us to the next village and carried his daughter into the guest house. She was very sick with pneumonia. Her breathing was already a death rattle. We did everything we could, gave her medicines and infusions and finally turned to the father and gave him enough medicines to last several days. But I knew they wouldn't help. I knew that little girl couldn't possible live. And she was only about three!

A doctor has to face that kind of failure, time and again. But that night I was tired. I felt discouraged. It seemed to me that in the face of the millions who needed our help, we were able to do such a very little.

Then I thought of something the former dean of my medical school had said to me: "Tom, you will face periods of abject discouragement—every doctor does. You will feel then that all your efforts are pitifully small in the face of the bigness of your task. But remember, Tom, all the big steps in the progress of humanity can be traced back to the individual. So keep up your courage, and as Saint Paul said so many years ago, 'Be steadfast in faith.' "

The next morning we got into our boats again and started on a new day's work. That night we spent in a Kha Kho village. The Kha Kho tribal women wear heavy rings in their ears; often their ear lobes are only yawning holes circled by a string of stretched flesh. These support huge, egg-sized knobs of gold or silver which represent their life savings. The Kha Kho men often have a wispy, black mustache, no more than a hundred hairs. These drop from the corners of their mouths. They look like Tartar tribesmen but they have soft eyes that make you think of Asian holy men.

In this village we were met with real suspicion. Every child had a flourishing case of whooping cough. You could hear their hacking all night long. We had plenty of tetramycyn, the cure for this disease, and we dosed the children with it. After a sleepless night, we packed up our things, loaded it into the boats, and started off again down the river.

That night we stopped off at Ban Pak Tha, a village

that is built on a lush piece of land at a point where the Nam Tha River joins the mighty Mekong. This village was small, but it had something about it that was dignified. The village chief escorted us to a big, termite-infested house that must once have been quite beautiful. But years of monsoons, disuse and tropical ravages had nearly reduced it to the dust from which it came. To our eyes, however, it looked like Buckingham Palace.

After dinner that night we held a sick call which lasted till midnight. A boy called Kieu was substituting for Chai as interpreter on this river trip. He was a good enough sort but he was terribly worried about "face." On this particular night, I must admit I was tired and cross. And the crowds at sick call kept closing in on me so tightly that I could hardly breathe, much less listen to a chest through a stethoscope.

I told Kieu to ask the crowd to move back, as I was being suffocated. He said something in his gentle, ineffectual way but no one moved. I told him again, a little sharply, to get the mob back. I was really getting a little frightened. He repeated something in a low voice. Nothing happened. Finally I turned and yelled at him to get those people to move back or I would stop sick call. I had no idea that yelling at my interpreter would cause him to lose that much face. But it did.

Kieu just walked away and refused to work. John went after him, to try to apologize for me and get him to come back, but he could not, for he would lose face! So we had to hold sick call that night without him.

The next morning we changed boats. We were now nearing civilization on the Mekong. Here there were larger boats that had motors on them. These haul rice up and down the river. We were able to get a place on one of these on top of several tons of burlap rice bags. We left all our remaining medicines with the school-teacher at Ban Pak Tha. So with just our personal belongings we departed for Luang Prabang, the old religious capital of Laos.

On the afternoon of the eighth day we were still sprawling amidst the howling livestock, nursing mothers, sweating coolies and dried meats of this Mekong *Queen Mary,* when Kieu, now restored to good humor, came to tell us that we would soon be arriving at Luang Prabang. We climbed up on to the roof of our boat and watched the beautiful, ancient city loom into view. The first thing we saw was the high, golden spire of the main pagoda.

As soon as the crew got a piece of planking down, we scrambled off the boat and climbed up the bank to the road. Here, with the solid earth beneath us, we felt that the river trip was at last completed. Those last days spent amidst the isolated villages seemed more fruitful to us than the whole preceding month. We really had taken American humanity into the most unknown, untouched hinterlands. We felt as if we had done a worthwhile service in the name of our country, our fellow man and our God.

On our second afternoon in Luang Prabang, we decided to pay our respects to the Viceroy of Laos, His Highness Prince Phetserath. The Prince had not always been pro-American in his comments, but he was deeply interested in his people and he showed it. He had sent us a present of some husky chickens of fine breed from Thailand.

The Prince received us in his beautiful palace that lies amidst lovely gardens on a bend of the river. The Prince was tremendously interested in our trip and in the sicknesses we had met with. He asked about hospital problems and wanted to know how much it was costing for rice per patient.

I seized the opportunity to tell the Prince a little about my plans. I told him that my money was almost gone now, that in August my two assistants would have to go back to Notre Dame to begin the fall semester. I explained that we had trained some of the local people and that we hoped they would take over from us. Laughingly, I said that I had come to give aid to the Lao and had succeeded in working myself out of a job.

"Good," said the Prince.

I must admit the remark took me somewhat by surprise. When he saw this the Prince explained, "That is what aid should be, doctor. It should not make people more dependent on the aider, or upon the country from which he comes. Aid, ideally, should work itself into a position where it does away with any further need of itself."

After thinking this over, I agreed with the Prince.

As we left, the Prince walked out of his palace and took us down to our jeep. Holding out his hand in democratic fashion, he turned to us. "Thank you for what you have done for my people," he said, "and come back soon!"

The way he said it made me happy and proud of the work we had been able to do.

CHAPTER THIRTEEN

Back at Nam Tha Again

Back at Nam Tha again, we were soon sucked into the old life. It was monotonous and it was wretched, but we were doing the work we wanted to do. Weeks and months passed. Hideous skin diseases, filth, dysentery, leprosy—these were our daily visitors. But now the children with their pus-filled eyes, wearing rags for clothes, underfed and pitiful, had become "our" children; their problems had become "our" problems. When they improved we felt better too, when they thanked us this was our pay. And when we felt a certain rich sense of satisfaction with even a small accomplishment, we knew that God was telling us that He was pleased with our work.

Each morning I walked into the hospital compound with the feeling that I was traveling backward in time to a disease-ridden world that had ceased to exist long before I was born. In medical school, the professors had said, "We can now look upon leprosy, gentlemen, as a disease that belonged to the Biblican era—we may say that the terrors of diphtheria, typhoid and smallpox vanished with the coming of modern vaccine therapy. . . ."

113

Ah yes, professors! But here they all are—with others even more terrible—crowded into my own waiting room, here at Nam Tha. They are the commonplace problems of any average day. This is Asia in the twentieth century. But not the twentieth century that western man knows!

Sometimes the health problems we had to deal with were due to simple ignorance. The people of Laos have grown so used to disease that they accept it as a normal part of living. They speak of *kia tamada,* "normal fever." And they have lived on the edge of starvation for so long that their bodies have lost the ability to store vitamins, fats and proteins. Even a few days of illness can throw their starved systems into a negative balance.

We pumped them full of vitamins and passed out quantities of the wonderful MPF that Meals for Millions had given us. The medicines did their work and word got around that we were curing people. The result of this "fame" was that I was swamped with work.

But surgery was my heaviest burden. Scarcely a day passed without its quota of emergencies—a man who had been mauled by a bear; a child whose hand had been blown off while playing with a live cartridge left over from the war; a worker who had practically chopped off a foot while cutting bamboo in the jungle. My operating schedule grew longer by the day.

Once a man appeared with a wife who had a tumor the size of a tangerine hanging from her lower lip. The husband begged me to remove it. I had never performed that kind of an operation before and I had only the vaguest idea of the procedure as it was described in the textbooks. But the growth was already infected, and infections on the face are terribly dangerous. I decided to try.

Some weeks later we discharged the woman, healed and happy. The husband looked upon it as a miracle. Later I learned that he was the mayor of a village some miles distant. That man did a lot to spread the word that the white medicine men in Nam Tha were to be counted among Buddha's blessings.

Wild animals were responsible for many bad wounds. The wild boar, a common inmate of the jungle all around us, was extremely dangerous. When a boar sees a person, instead of running away, he will always lunge right at him. To hunt the boars the Lao find a narrow clear strip like a trail or a path. Then the villagers form a line and, almost shoulder to shoulder, walk through the jungle beating their drums and yelling. The boar runs ahead; finally he crosses the cleared path. There, up in a tree, the hunter sits with an old musket or flintlock.

One man had not yet climbed up the tree when a boar lumbered out of the jungle into the clearing. As soon as he saw the man, he attacked. The boar is the size of a very large hog and he has two vicious curled teeth that are sometimes eight inches long. The animal immediately downed the native and sank his teeth deep into the man's thigh. The leg was impaled on the curled fangs and as the boar shook his head, he threw the man about, ripping the flesh off the leg. Finally the screaming man managed to tear himself loose. The boar kept slashing with his teeth until finally other villagers came and drove him away.

By the time the wounded man reached us, he had almost bled to death. His right hand was mutilated beyond repair. We managed to save the leg. Months later he came to visit us, walking with only a slight limp. As for his right hand, it healed all right, but was partially paralyzed.

Late one afternoon four Thai Dam tribesmen arrived in Nam Tha in a state of collapse. They had two poles on their shoulders and hanging from these was a roughly made litter. On top was a thin mattress and nearly hidden beneath cotton blankets was a head of hair and the gaunt face of a young boy. His friends and his brother had carried this boy down from a village several days away. How they managed to get that crude stretcher across the wild mountains and through the dense jungle is something I will never understand. They set their pitiful load down in front of our hospital and we went out to examine the child.

The first thing we noticed was that he was infested with lice. He had head lice in his hair and scabies over his whole body. As we pulled the cloth blankets off him, we saw a horrible sight. This boy looked like a man who had recently escaped from a concentration camp. His whole body was contorted with pain and frozen in a twisted position. He had a deep, long-standing muscle infection of the left leg. Because he had to lie on his mat of a bed and never move, all the rest of his body had wasted away. His left leg, the good leg, was no bigger around the thigh than my wrist is. He was so filthy that even as he lay there, the flies began to crawl over his face, around his lips and into his eyes and ears. His brother kept trying to brush the flies away.

We agreed to keep the boy, Nai, in the hospital but our first condition was that he go down to the river and be thoroughly scrubbed. We gave him a shampoo that kills body lice and some ointment that will clear up even a bad case of scabies. After a thorough washing with soap—the first in his life—we admitted him into the ward.

The boys built an orthopedic bed for Nai. It had teak-wood posts around it with a frame overhead. From this frame hung a trapeze bar. With the help of antibiotics and surgery, the infection cleared up in a few days. The fight was now physiotherapy. Nai had many months of exercise ahead of him. We taught him how to do various exercises which helped to restore his muscle strength. His heel tendons were almost frozen in a position which made his toe point straight out, and he could not bend his foot upwards. His younger brother stayed on at the hospital and took care of him. This boy learned how to do all the exercises. He spent most of his time devotedly moving his brother's arms and legs up and down, and also kept urging Nai to try to do it himself. It was wonderful to see the strong family love that exists among these primitive people.

Months later, on a cane that his brother made for him, Nai could stand alone at the side of his bed. Soon he walked around the bed, although he still had to clutch at the wooden frame. Later he could get across the ward and one day he called to me. He had walked across the compound and stood before us at the main building as proud as any boy in the world could be. And we were proud of him, too! Nai had won the battle against his disease; with his own will he had forced his muscles to work again. A few weeks later, the boy who had come to us near death returned to his village. He held his head high, walked straight and well, and was neatly dressed in American khakis.

The force of kindness and love shown by my boys and his own brother, had rescued Nai from a tragic life. It is my belief that faith in this force is the greatest bond among nations. An Asian brother and some American helpers, both taking care of a stricken boy, had taught him to walk again. Kindness is close to God and disarms man the quickest. You will never find this boy or his brothers fighting against an American. They will always remember us with love.

We had hundreds of patients like Nai whom we could cure. And, unhappily, we had other patients to whom we could not even offer a breath of chance.

But life at Nam Tha was not always grim. Sometimes we had fun, too. One of the great events for us was the day we introduced something astonishing into the lives of the village kids. We held a track meet! The head of the village school helped us make our plans. We had three-legged races, fifty yard dashes, tug-of-wars and other games. For prizes we gave out every Hershey bar, pencil and calendar we owned. We even had some propaganda photos of the King of Laos. These we awarded to the top winners. Then each child had his picture taken with our Polaroid camera as a lasting memento of his day of glory.

The anti-white man propaganda that the Communists were feeding so cleverly into all these villages along the China border, was partly dissolved in our "miracle medicines." But I believe that our track meets, village parties, movies and rough-housing with the children, helped just as much.

While in Laos, all of us learned to speak the language

of the country, not exactly fluently, but enough to make ourselves understood. Medical Lao is very simple. The word *chep* means "pain." *Li* means "lots of," or the superlative of anything. The longer the word is dragged out, and the higher the pitch of the voice, the more intense the meaning. All one has to do is learn the words for the parts of the body, or just watch the patient point to his head and listen to his *chep hua liiiiii*. Although we all reached the stage where we could understand most medical problems and express ourselves well enough in the clinic, we still didn't do very well when we went to dinner with the Governor. For example the word *cai* can mean "chicken," "egg," "fever," "far away," or "nearby" —all according to the tone used, and the length or brevity of the word. You can see how embarrassing this can get.

One of our best sources of amusement was the dirty, brown kids. They were around all through the day and most of the night, staring at us in fascination. What they liked especially was to watch us eat. Our diet was a mixture of East and West. We ate their scrawny chickens and eggs, along with our regular C-rations. We downed our canned meat drowned in their fish sauce. Once we even tried tiger steaks, but they tasted like old shoes.

We always loved to open packages and everyone enjoyed watching us. It took hours to open everything we might receive at one mail call. We would go over the medical samples, the instruments, vitamin pills, Hershey bars and magazines. We learned that it is not necessary to have cigarettes, a bar or a movie or a TV set. The simple things of life can give us happiness.

The physical layout of our living in Nam Tha was

better than at Vang Vieng. It had to be because the conditions in which we lived were ten times worse. Nam
Tha was a village in medieval times. We had to work
constantly to keep our house in "livable condition." We
had to keep repainting, rescrubbing, rebuilding, all the
time. One afternoon the whole lower side of a wall fell
out. These walls are made from woven bamboo, then a
mixture like wattle is made from cow dung, rice straw,
betel juice, lime and other ingredients known only to
God and the natives. This paste is then spread on each
side of the bamboo. The overall effect is a sort of smelly
adobe.

Lots of people say that the Lao are a lazy people. But
from my own experience of living like a Lao, in a hut
like his own, I wish to say that this is not true. Let me
tell you of just a few things a Lao man must do. He must
forge the iron, make and repair his plow, carving the
yoke and the shaft himself. He must constantly rebuild
his harrow and blade. He must repair his house, weave
new walls, cut thatch for the roof, repair his kitchen tools.
He must keep his cart, feed his oxen, make rope and
fiber. He must make hemp and weave the nets, then fish
for his meals. He must build a loom so that his wife and
daughter can weave. But first he must grow, gin, mill
and dye, the cotton. He must take care of his sick buffalo,
till his fields, practice his religion and raise chickens and
ducks and grow a garden.

And then there is the fight against the bugs. To keep
them from swarming over everything is a job all by itself. We found that it was impossible to do surgery at
night because of the teeming swarms of insects of all
kinds. When emergencies forced us to do it, the bugs

would swirl around the light, climb into our hair and faces, even to the wound. Nets, screens, nothing we could contrive would keep them out. The air would be absolutely solid with insects. We had to turn our kerosene lamps out on some nights because the bugs left us no other choice.

It was a rewarding life, but not always an easy one. Even with the sense of humor we tried to keep going, loneliness gnawed at us all the time. We were so close to the Chinese border that there were few people who were willing to take a chance of getting marooned if they came to see us. But on two occasions during our stay at Nam Tha, we were visited by an Oblate missionary.

John, Bob and I are Catholics. It meant a lot to us to see our hut transformed into a Church of God during the thirty minutes that the priest offered Holy Mass. I have attended Masses in the most magnificent cathedrals of the world, in many of the countries on this earth. I've heard sermons in most of the languages of Europe and several of Asia. But never did the words seem to take on such meaning, never was there such a profound depth to this meaning, as when a small French missionary genuflected before our table-transformed-into-an-altar, and said, "I shall go unto the altar, to the altar of my God. . .".

It is sometimes hard to see God in all things when you are plunged into a brash materialism. It is easier in the jungle. Here we can know God a little better. Perhaps it is because of the solitude. But here we see God in the tropic rain, in the monsoon mud, in the tangy, sweet smell of the earth that comes upon us as we walk alone among the mountains. The mimosa, the tamarind trees, the thatched roof, the peace, the coolness of the river, the surge of the night, all of these can mean so much if we listen and seek Him. All we need do is listen to the voices inside us, listen more acutely, rub our eyes and see things a little better. If the light is seen, if the sound is heard, then a man's whole being is caught up in soul-satisfying contentment.

One thing has become very clear to me. A man who works in this world and doesn't tap his own reservoir of spiritual strength is like a twin-engined plane flying with only one motor. He may reach his goal, but it will be mighty difficult. Often, late at night, Bob, John, and I would kneel beside our cots and pray the family rosary out loud. Our whole job took on a new meaning when we remembered the words, "Inasmuch as ye have done it unto the least of these, my brethren, ye have done it unto me."

CHAPTER FOURTEEN

Handing on the Torch

I had been in Laos over a year: time was running out. Funds were running low, too. Baker had gone home in January, Denny Shepard in March, Peter Kessey in May. If John de Vitry and Bob Waters were to reach Notre Dame in time for the fall semester they, too, must leave for home. Operation Laos was nearing the end. Soon I would be going home myself—but not quite yet. I still had something to do.

For some time I had been turning things over in my mind and now I had some proposals to make to the Minister of Health. We had established a hospital; it must continue to serve the people of Nam Tha even after we left. I was very eager to have the Government of Laos take over the work we had begun.

The words Prince Phetserath had spoken, kept echoing and reëchoing through my mind: "Aid should not make people more dependent on the aider. Aid should work itself into a position where it abolishes any further need of itself."

Help on a people-to-people basis, it seems to me, is a sort of relay race. You light a torch and run the course;

then you hand on your torch to the next man on the team. Our whole work at Nam Tha had been planned with that end in view. It was for this reason that we did not install X-ray machines or build any large electrical plant. It was for this reason that we used no complicated instruments or any very delicate apparatus. The people of Laos must be able to carry on after we had gone home. So that the local nurses would have no difficulty in understanding the use and dosage of antibiotics, we had made it a point only to use ten or twelve of the basic ones. We had turned over our CARE kits to the midwives and taught the locals about vaccination. They would carry on our work long after we were back in the United States.

We had succeeded in building something. I did not want what we had accomplished to fade away after we left. So when my boys had to leave for the capital to catch their plane for home, I went down with them.

We arrived safely in Vientiane and a few days later I put John and Bob on their plane. That very morning I went to see the Minister of Health. I took with me a plan for the future of our hospital and a schedule for the "phasing out" stage of our work.

Dr. Oudom received me very cordially and after we had exchanged greetings, I got right down to what was closest to my heart. I had three points to propose:

1. I asked him to give our hospital a Lao charter. This meant he would see to it that a certain sum of money would be earmarked for the hospital. The amount of money would be based on the number of patients who were treated and hospitalized. In addition a certain sum would be set aside for upkeep and care of the buildings.

All the medicines used would come from the government warehouse.

2. I asked the Minister of Health to send Bangkok-trained nurses to Nam Tha to take the places of my men. There were only a very few well-trained nurses in the whole of Laos. But I asked for two for Nam Tha.

3. I asked that a *médecin indochinois* be sent to Nam Tha to replace me.

4. I told Dr. Oudum that if he would agree to my three points, I, in turn, would agree to leave everything that we had brought to Laos in the hospital at Nam Tha. This included beds, mosquito nets, linens, surgical instruments, stethoscopes, house gear and about $25,000 worth of antibiotics. All these would be turned over to the *médecin indochinois* and when that was done, I would myself return to America.

The Minister agreed at once to my conditions. He seemed surprised, however, that I wanted to become expendable. I told him that in my mind America should not try to make a foreign land dependent on her for its medical aid.

"But," Dr. Oudom asked, "are you really content to be replaced by a man who does not measure up to your ability as a doctor?"

I told him that I believed the *médecin indochinois* was the best medical officer the Lao government had, and that I would be very pleased if he would take over what we had built. Then, I added, "But I hope you are not too pleased at my going. Because I hope to come back to Laos again."

Dr. Oudom smiled. "You and your men have worn the cotton strings of the *Baci*. The heart of the Lao people is in your hands. You may return whenever you wish."

Shortly after our talk, I left for the north to set the six weeks' phase-out period in motion. At Nam Tha most of the village came to meet my plane.

The "new doctor" had already arrived and we had a long talk. I urged him to let the patients pay for their medicines, as we had done. Operation Laos had never been a charity program. The people of Laos are proud and they are pleased to pay for what they get. The Lao doctor agreed with me. He also had some good ideas of his own. One of the first things he did was to start the villagers building a large fence around the hospital compound to keep the water buffalo from wandering around the front lawn of the surgical ward. I wondered why I had never thought of that!

The young Lao doctor ran the sick call line every day now; I would only go over around noon to see the cases on which he wished my opinion. In the afternoons we would do surgery. The villagers knew that the "new" doctor had come to replace me and that the two new nurses were the replacements for John and Bob. When they seemed worried by the new state of affairs, I did all I could to transfer to the new doctor the confidence and trust we had won after a year in this country. He would need it.

Every day villagers and mountain tribesmen came to my house to give me going-away gifts. They would ask me how far it was to my village in America and when I was coming back to Nam Tha. Even the old witch doctors came to say goodbye. The teller of old legends came and wished me all happiness. He said that he hoped a butterfly would perch on my shoulder and that this good omen would bring me happiness. An old sorceress came and sat before me and shook her joss sticks in their cylinders. She threw the half moon clappers on the ground before me and said that my future looked bright, and in it she could see my return to her village.

The Governor gave a going-away party for me. The villagers attended in full force. A *Lam Vong*, the national dance of Laos, was held. A platform was built in the village square, and the amplifier from our movie projector was used for the local orchestra of drums, khenes, and string instruments. During the previous year, whenever a *Lam Vong* had been held, you could always find the Dooley mission there. Tonight I was alone.

On the morning of my departure hundreds and hundreds of villagers were milling around the strip as I walked out with Si and Chai. Only last February, I had walked down this same landing strip, but how different the people looked to me now. I knew each one of them, I remembered their sufferings, I had been part of their lives. As I walked through the crowd many reached out and thanked me with a simple touch that said more than any words.

These people had become important to me. I had learned to love them.

The plane took off. When we were in the air the hard-boiled French pilot turned to me and said, *"Ils vous aiment bien."* Yes, I believe they did love me too.

CHAPTER FIFTEEN

MEDICO

On a bleak November day, I stood in the lobby of the Mayflower Hotel in Washington, D.C., waiting impatiently to have lunch with a man whom I did not know. But in spite of the fact that I had never met him, I felt that we were friends, for we had been writing to each other for nearly a year. This man was Dr. Peter Comanduras, a distinguished Washington doctor and an associate professor of Clinical Medicine at the George Washington University Medical School.

I looked at my watch, paced up and down the lobby. I had a strong hunch that this luncheon meeting was going to be important for me, or rather for my work. After fifteen months of field work I knew that something I had always believed in theory was a practical reality. I had seen that compassion and gentleness can build a bridge that is strong enough to link nation to nation. I had learned that we, Americans, possess a weapon that is more powerful than any bomb yet invented—the force of simple human gentleness and love.

This was something I wanted to say to all my fellow Americans. But most of all I wanted to say it to Dr. Comanduras. Why? Because, of all the letters I received while I was in Laos—and there were thousands of them—his letters had been the most sympathetic and the most inspiring. It seemed to me that we were two people who could speak to each other heart to heart.

Then a handsome man in his early fifties walked into the lobby and headed straight for me: it was Dr. Comanduras. We went in to lunch and as we talked, I began to understand the bond that had made our correspondence such a heart-warming experience. Dr. Comanduras was passionate in his conviction of the special form American medical aid to foreign nations must take. He believed as I did that work of this kind should be done by individual doctors and that they must be free of government control. We believed basically that we should come as visitors; that we should build and stock a small hospital, train the villagers to run the hospital on a simple level, and after a few years—two, three or four—turn the hospital over to the people of the country. For Dr. Comanduras, as for me, the vital point in this medical aid on a people-to-people basis was to keep things simple.

After a while I produced figures to show that our sixteen months' mission had cost less than $50,000, plus the drugs and supplies that had been given to us.

Dr. Comanduras was delighted. He turned to me, his eyes shining so that his face looked young under his greying hair. "I feel pretty much as you do, Dooley," he said. "How can we go around preaching this idea to others unless we are willing to go out and practice it ourselves? I have been thinking seriously, you know, of giving up my commitments here and taking up this work myself."

Then and there we decided that there had been enough talk. The time had come to do something. Something simple and positive. Dr. Comanduras told me he had tried and failed to sell his common sense approach to foreign aid officials. We decided to approach the International Rescue Committee.

A week later, I stood in the board room of the IRC and faced a group of their distinguished directors. I gave them a report on Operation Laos, then I sat down and waited.

"Well, doctor," someone asked, "what exactly do you propose that we should do?"

"From the modest beginnings I have made," I said, "I propose that we carry the work another step further. I believe I have shown that a medical team like mine can be kept in the field for sixteen months on a budget of $50,000.

"Dr. Comanduras and I have drawn up a plan for sending six such teams into the field. My own team will return to Laos, the other five will be sent into other critical areas.

"I propose, gentlemen, that this plan be adopted by the International Rescue Committee."

For a moment there was silence. Then several people began to talk at once. Most of the board members, it turned out, were for my plan. The idea of medical work done on a simple, human basis with no strings attached, appealed to everyone. The only hitch was that this work did not fit the charter of the IRC.

"We would have to change our charter," someone objected.

I jumped to my feet. "Why not?" I blithely asked.

They all laughed goodnaturedly at my brashness. But they began to discuss the point. At last a motion was made to amend the charter so that the IRC could "accept the task of providing humanitarian medical aid to threatened parts of the world."

That was the birth of MEDICO—officially, Medical International Cooperation.

It was inspiring to watch the medical profession rally to our support. Doctors and dentists sacrificed thriving practices to volunteer for this work of bringing simple medical care to the poorest of the poor, the neediest of the needy, all over the world. Nurses, technicians, social workers and plain college students like John de Vitry and Bob Waters were eager to serve on our teams. Dr. Comanduras was elected our Secretary General. Although we were originally launched under the auspices of the International Rescue Committee, we later became an independent organization—Medico, Inc.—wholly on our own.

A month before, en route home from Laos, I had sat beside Dr. Albert Schweitzer on the banks of the Ogowe River in French Equatorial Africa. I have never forgotten what that great man said to me so simply that night: "The significance of a man, Doctor Tom, is not in what he attains but rather in what he longs to attain."

It seemed to me now that MEDICO was born out of that talk. We were all going to do our best to make something we believed in come true. We hoped to succeed; we must be prepared to fail. Only one thing was completely sure: what we were "longing to attain" was something that was big and fine; something that might deserve to be called the brotherhood of man. This was what Dr. Schweitzer had been doing in Africa, so triumphantly and in such a lonely way, for so many years.

That night I sat down and wrote Dr. Schweitzer a letter. I pointed out to him that through MEDICO Americans could show the world, not only how Americans will care for and help other men, but how men can help other men. I asked him to accept a position he has never been willing to accept before in all his eighty-five years of living. I asked him to accept the position of Honorary Patron of MEDICO.

The proudest statement I can make and the best endorsement MEDICO could have, is that Dr. Albert Schweitzer has accepted.

CHAPTER SIXTEEN

Muong Sing

High up in the northwest corner of Laos, only six miles from the Red China border, nestled in a lush green valley surrounded by mountains covered by a great rainforest, is a cluster of thatched huts threaded by a few streets that are knee-deep in filth and garbage. Chickens, pigs, cows, water-buffalo and dirty, tattered human beings roam the streets in indescribable confusion. This is Muong Sing, the village selected by the Royal Government of Laos as the site of a hospital to be sponsored by MEDICO and run by Dr. Tom Dooley. We arrived in September 1958, only six months after the birth of MEDICO.

Working with me this time were two new American volunteers, Earl Rhine ("Rhine like the river," he always says) and Dwight Davis. Earl, though born in Illinois, had lived in Texas long enough to become "Texan," and Dwight was Texan by right of birth. Like Norman Baker, Earl and Dwight had served an apprenticeship in the Navy, and both were working at Brackenridge Hospital in Austin, Texas when they read an article in Life Magazine about the Dooley mission. Then and there they decided that this was the kind of work they wanted to do. The two had been friends for several years and that was one of the reasons I chose them out of all the hundreds who applied. I figured that when I got angry with one of them, he could always go to his friend for comfort. Earl and Dwight were still in their twenties, both had brown hair and brown eyes and both were devoted to their calling, body and soul.

I did not believe that the lives of the villagers of Muong Sing would form a hinge of history. But I did believe that their lives were important, as life itself is important. Each human being is important just because he is a human being. I tried to get this idea across to Earl and Dwight, only to find that both of them already held this same view of life. Whether a child at our hospital was a ragged mountain boy or the son of the local mayor, he was important to my boys just because he was a child.

We were hard at work from the very first day we arrived. First we cleaned up the house in which we were to live, then the clinic. When that was finished we went to work on the new ward building. About fifty yards behind the clinic was the shell of a small building. Attached to this on three sides was a series of grass huts housing the wives of some of the local soldiers. Gently but very firmly, we had these ladies evicted, then we took over the area for our wards. The huts were torn off, a wall or two was knocked down, another built up. After a bout of hectic activity during which we cemented, scrubbed, whitewashed and painted, we were in possession of a three-room ward with "mat space" for twenty or twenty-five patients. We covered all the holes in the walls with postcards that had been sent us by wellwishers from all over the world.

Seeing us so active, our patients decided to go in for a little painting on their own. They decorated their walls with homemade murals in which the signs and symbols of "black magic" figured prominently. Like the people of Nam Tha, the villagers at Muong Sing believed firmly in witchcraft and sorcery. Every mountain had its legend, every valley its myth and there were as many herbs in their pharmacopoeia as there were trees in the forest. Once again we were forced to make friends with the sorcerers and our hospital walls testified to our peaceful coexistence, but this was not new to me.

The Lao army sent a working party to help us with our building. The whole compound was leveled off and what had been a patchwork of sink holes, buffalo wallows, ditches and hillocks became a level, clean hospital compound. We even planted grass, then fenced in the whole area with barbed wire. Earl, with the know-how of a midwestern farmer, set out a vegetable garden. Our tomatoes grew to be big and juicy but we never got a chance to eat them. The jungle monkeys got there first! Si, who returned to work with me again, planted flowers and soon we had a good-looking compound, a little on the primitive side, perhaps, but neat and clean.

When everything was finished, our ward was truly unique. We had three rooms which we dignified with the titles of "Ward A," "Ward B" and "Ward C." Each room was fourteen feet wide and about as long as two American beds placed end to end with an aisle between them. On each side of the door as you entered was a platform and at the opposite end of the room, there was another platform. When we had equipped these with bamboo mats and mosquito nets, the patients slept on them, five or six to each platform.

If you made the rounds on a typical day, you saw something like this: On Mat 1, Ward A, a small girl of the Kha Mou tribe sick with pneumonia. Her mother, a surgical case, was with her. We treated both of them.

On Mat 4, lay an old man from high up in the mountains. We had removed a stone from his bladder about the size of a tennis ball. This old man was the grateful type. "Doctor American" he said generously, "you can have my stone. I don't want it."

On another part of the same platform sat a small boy who was nearly blind in both eyes. Constant infections had scarred his eyelids and the scars made the eyelids turn inside out. This caused more scars and more infections. If he hadn't come to us to be operated on, he would have become totally blind by the time he was ten. After surgery and a followup treatment with cortisone drops, he was able to see as well as any normal child.

Walking out of the door and down the porch into Ward B we could see a small boy whose name was Guntar. Guntar belonged to the Kha Kho tribe and claimed to be seven years old. By the Buddhist calendar this might have been true; by our calendar he was closer to six. A few weeks before Guntar's father had shot a tiger that was prowling near their jungle home. In wild excitement the child had run up to the "dead" tiger. But the animal was still alive enough to lunge at him, mauling him and practically tearing off his leg. At first we thought we would have to amputate the already gangrenous limb, but antibiotics plus good, old-fashioned TLC ("tender, loving care") saved the day.

Little Guntar loved the movie we showed at night with the wall of our house serving as a screen. Walt Disney had given us a 16mm. version of Dumbo and that wonderful elephant proved to have as much healing power as our antibiotics. All the children of Muong Sing were Dumbo fans. "What a wonderful land America must be," they said. "You have elephants that are pink and green and purple. And some of them have ears so big they can fly through the air."

Our wards were always full up. Some of our patients had dysentery, malaria, skin diseases and malnutrition. These we could cure. But there were others with leprosy and some with bad cases of tuberculosis that were beyond our help. Then there were still others who, while they would never be completely well again, could at least be helped with treatments and diet instructions, so that they could go to their homes again and lead fairly normal lives.

Every morning, just a little after dawn, Dwight and Earl made the ward rounds. I made rounds only in the afternoon when I would see just those cases that Earl and Dwight felt unable to manage alone. Often I watched them at their work and was proud of them.

Earl had a gentle tact that never deserted him. One day a wizened old man came to him to be treated. With gestures worthy of an accomplished actor, he tried to make Earl understand about the terrible pain that was attacking him. "It begins in my left knee," he said, "and runs up the inside of my leg. Then it plunges into my pelvis and continues up to my face and into my head. After that it comes out the tip of my nose until it falls into my knee, the other one."

Earl listened very attentively, nodding his head and

looking solemn. At last he said, "Oh yes, of course. I understand perfectly. I suggest hot soaks for both knees."

Dwight had a gay way with his patients. He jokingly called all the haggard old gals "honey," at the same time examining them with an attention worthy of a queen. Both my men were magnificent. The only risk the patients ran at their hands was an overdose of compassion.

Almost as soon as I reached Laos this time, I began to hear rumors that things were not going well at Nam Tha. According to my informants, the new *médecin indochinois* who had taken my place was inadequate and the hospital was now poorly run. I was urged on all sides to go right over to Nam Tha and straighten things out.

I refused. A man must practice what he preaches. And for years I had been preaching that the whole function of foreign medical aid is to start a hospital, get it in good running order, then turn it over to the native government involved. The hospital at Nam Tha was close to my heart, I could never lose interest in it, but I had turned it over to the Lao government and I no longer felt that I had any rights there. The Nam Tha hospital was now a Lao responsibility and a Lao problem.

I believed that if enough Lao heard about the situation there, they would do something about it. And in time that is exactly what did happen.

When a new doctor had taken over and everything was in good shape again at Nam Tha and my own hospital at Muong Sing was running smoothly, I decided that at last the time had come for me to go and say "hello" to my old friends. So one day Earl and I packed up some spare equipment and nearly 1,000 pounds of medicines and set off for Nam Tha. The Lao government sent an Army DC-3 for us. I was grateful for the lift, for although Nam Tha is not far from Muong Sing as the crow flies, it is a long day's journey away if you go by land.

It was a bittersweet feeling to be in Nam Tha again. As I walked through the once familiar village, my mind was flooded with old memories. Here we had worked all night to save a burnt child, there the villagers had given a dance for us. I even met the old lady who had always honored me with that betel-stained smile. She was still smiling.

My old nurses gave a big party for us. Everything was going well under the direction of the new doctor. By American standards the Nam Tha hospital was on the primitive side, but I can never believe that air-conditioning, electricity and fancy equipment are the most important things. The vital ingredient in a hospital is compassion. And the Nam Tha hospital had plenty of that.

Some of our former students were living in our old house. They had made a few "improvements." Where Eisenhower's picture used to hang during our reign, a photograph of the King of Laos now held sway. The green paint had turned a sort of greenish brown and the whole place was a little dirtier than when we lived in it. But I had been sitting on the old porch only a few minutes when old friends came crowding in to see me.

Ion, the boy who had been so terribly burned that he nearly died and whose charred flesh had been covered with maggots, was now quite grown up. He was well and strong and his smile was as enchanting as ever. Ion brought me a present, just as he had done every day two years before. This time it was three eggs and a coconut.

Old Maggie, the village sorceress, arrived too, the same dirty towel still wrapped around her head. We did not discuss the newest antibiotics, but we did have a good reunion. I gave her a can of shaving cream for a present. No, she doesn't shave, but the soap comes out of the aerosol in such a magic way. And if she puts the soap on any wounds she may be treating, it will be a lot more sanitary than her usual betel-juice-baboon-blood-uric-acid concoction.

One of the villages that used to be on our old jeep call route invited us over for a banquet. When we arrived we found tables twenty-five feet long set out for us. They were laden with wooden bowls, heaped high with food. The dinner was given in the house of the village chief and to do us honor the floor had been covered with leaves and palm branches. On top of the leaves stood silver bowls filled with assorted meats and vegetables. In their desire to give us a fine welcome the villagers had assembled every imaginable thing to eat—and a few that were distinctly unimaginable. There were pigs' feet, bat wings, tripe, fish sauces, buffalo steaks and various herbs, both the sweet-smelling variety and the other kind. There was also the usual limp-looking salad, the one my boys had christened the "dysentery dish." There were in addition raw frogs, assorted insects, fried beetles, cooked tree bark and roots, and some very thin sparrow carcasses. But the *pièce de résistance* was served in a hand-hammered silver bowl which stood in the very center of the longest table: a brew of nice, warm, freshly-congealed pig blood!

We stayed late. It was wonderful to feel the warm comradeship of these old friends. Some of them had brought their babies to see me—the babies we had delivered. Former surgical patients dropped in at their chief's hut to show me how well their scars had healed or their bones knit. Many of the villagers asked for news of Johnny and Bob, many wanted to know whether Pete had managed to put on any weight yet. I felt like a country doctor, home again after a long absence, meeting all his old patients at the County Fair. Seeing his old patients happy and well gives a doctor an inner joy that is quiet and good. He has helped them to regain their health, and that is his best reward.

Feeling the warmth and the friendship these villagers showered on me, made me think of something else too. I remembered the hundreds and hundreds of people we had treated, the thousands more that had seen us. And I knew that we had left something with these Laos that was more precious even than health. In our small way we had helped to dispel some of their fears, some of their ignorance and some of their prejudice against that strange, powerful land across the seas from which we came.

And it seemed to me that in serving these poor people in far-off Laos, we had been privileged also to serve America. And that gave me a good feeling too.

CHAPTER SEVENTEEN

The Mark of Pain

One morning at Muong Sing, a Kha Kho tribesman was brought down to us from the mountains. Eight of his friends had carried him down the steep trail on a home-made stretcher. His upper arm had been completely torn off by a shot and his chest and abdomen were peppered with lead. The wound had been wrapped in monkey skin and packed with tobacco and dung. Naturally it was badly infected. We shot the patient full of anti-malarials and vitamins, gave him a thorough bath and then some intravenous infusions of glucose and proteins. Finally we put him on the operating table. Dwight gave him the anaesthetic and Earl, although he was himself laid low with a mild case of infectious hepatitis, came over to the hospital to help me in the surgery. We managed to close the arm up all right but a few days later the suture line was torn open again by a swelling caused by a lymph obstruction.

A few weeks later a visiting surgeon helped me to do a skin graft that had about an 80% take. We heaved a sigh of relief. That Kha Kho boy, at any rate, was going to be all right.

When he was a little better we asked him how he had acquired his wound. He told us a not very believable story. He said that he had been hunting with a friend, that he had climbed up into a tree and that the friend had mistaken him for a bear and shot him.

We asked no more questions. This man came from a village close to the China border and we had heard that kind of tale from other frontier people before. We knew that most probably he had been trying to escape from China and had been shot by the frontier patrols. If he had admitted that he was a refugee, the police would have felt that they had to send him back to China.

During the past year alone, over 14,000 refugees had escaped into our small valley. As a result the government of China was furious and was accusing the Laos of aiding and abetting Chinese citizens to leave their country. Laos is a very small nation, Red China is a giant one. To avoid provoking their powerful neighbor, the Lao police in our area were ordering all refugees to return to their homeland. The desperate escapees knew well enough that this meant torture and certain death. So they invented hunting accidents like our poor young Kha Kho patient did.

As the weeks passed the rumors of war grew more and more threatening. There were "incidents" all along the border between China and Vietnam. Radio Hanoi and Radio Peiping stepped up their attacks on Laos. And against America, too. The words "imperialists" and "colonialist" appeared more and more often in the daily broadcasts and in March, 1959 even our own little medical program came under attack. We were accused of being spies. Propaganda is a frightening thing. If you say the same thing over and over again, day after day, month after month, year after year, people at last begin to believe the words they have heard repeated so often.

One day a Lao Minister said to me, "Dr. Dooley, Radio Peiping accuses you of espionage in North Laos. That's absurd, isn't it? You don't work for any American agencies, do you?"

The mere fact that he said "do you?" showed me that the radio attacks were making inroads on this man's trust in us. But the fact that those bigwigs in far away Peiping thought it necessary to try to force our small hospital to leave Laos, proved to me that we must be doing something worth while.

"U.S. secret agencies have set up organizations in Laos under the guise of running a village hospital," Radio Peiping ranted one day. "The United States is plotting to provoke conflict along the China-Laos border. Their intention is to create a pretext for armed intervention by the United States and the other aggressive blocs. They want to drag the Laos step by step into war."

Hearing these things said about us did not make us feel exactly safe. We decided to take it as just another occupational hazard. But it did increase the loneliness that was always with us, the loneliness that always attacks men who find themselves swinging far out beyond the boundaries of normal existence. Yet in a way this kind of loneliness can be a good thing. It lifts you above the dull routine of every day with its ever-present misery and the constant sight of pain that stifles and oppresses. It forces you to moments of sudden awareness. I loved these mountains and these people. And I loved my work. I believe that God has put us on this earth not merely to exist from day to day, but to use our time in the service of others. Because of this we worked harder than ever.

One day Chai and I were called to a border village to see a very sick man. While we were there, we were asked to visit a hut down the trail where two new refugees had just arrived, one of them critically ill. We were led to a small grass hut on stilts. It was rickety and unstable.

Inside we found an old man and his daughter. The little girl was called Nun Di and she belonged to the Chinese portion of the Thai Lu tribe that lived fifty miles inside China.

The girl was lying on her side amidst the usual filth, surrounded by various herbs and incense sticks. She was doubled up in acute agony. When I touched her hand, she tried to bite me like a frightened puppy and pulled away in fear. Nun Di had a massive infection of the hip joint; she was a sick and wretched little girl. As I could not talk to her, I sent Chai to find someone who could. We told the interpreter to say that she would have to be taken to the hospital at once so that we could incise and drain her leg under anaesthesia. If she didn't come with us, she would very probably die; if she did not die she would be hideously crippled for life.

I watched her face as the interpreter slowly and quietly relay my words. Nun Di began to tremble and cry; she became almost hysterical. I touched her hand to reassure her because I believe that the eloquence of touch is the warmest of all. She pulled her hand away. "No," she sobbed, "No-no-no!" She simply refused to come to our hospital. The interpreter warned her again that if she did not go, and go soon, she would surely die. "I don't care," she said, "I choose to die here. I do not want to die in your hospital."

Other villagers who knew me tried to persuade her to change her mind. She only sobbed and whimpered like a beaten dog and both she and her father kept repeating over and over, "No—no—no. We will not go to the hospital. It has an American doctor."

I went outside and sat on the front ladder of the hut while the Lao did their best to convince the family. At last Chai came outside and joined me. He explained that this was not just the usual fear of a hospital or of evil spirits. It had nothing to do with our competitor witchcraft. This little girl was simply frightened of the American monsters she had heard so much about.

In her village Communist Commissars had given hundreds of lectures about these American monsters and they had given the Dooley hospital program at Muong Sing a special workover. We were not doctors at all, we were American spies. "They do especially terrible things to little girls," the Communists had said. "They inject germs into the bodies of young people and they beat children who don't take their medicines."

After hours of persuasion, Nun Di at last consented to come to our jeep. But she would only come to our hospital if her father and half a dozen other people came with her. I carried her down the stairs myself. Her half-frail, half-bloated little body trembled convulsively.

We got her to the hospital and on to the operating table. We put her under anesthesia, drained her leg, pumped her full of antibiotics and moved her to the ward. For several days Nun Di remained a frightened little wraith. Then our medicines began to take effect.

Her temperature dropped, her pain disappeared and she began to realize that she was going to get well. On the fourth day both she and her father broke down and told me why they had been so fearful. They were sorry now, they knew they had been wrong.

Meanwhile in the north of Laos Communist rebels had succeeded in getting arms, uniforms—and orders—from North Viet Nam. Fighting broke out in two provinces. In Muong Sing we were terribly close to the point where Laos, China and Burma merge in the high rainforest. It looked now as if the war might spread to us.

The boys and I discussed what we should do in an emergency. Should we evacuate and abandon our hospital?

There was danger here, there was exertion and loneliness. But there were also moments that paid such rich rewards that they made up for all the rest. In the evening when the chaos and sadness and pain of the day gave way to the silence of the night, I would remember that humanity is God on earth and that a doctor's job is to cure sometimes, to relieve often and to comfort always. At such times I would think of the bridge of friendship that joined our hospital at Muong Sing to far-off America. And I thought, too, of Abraham Lincoln's words, "Freedom is for all men in all lands everywhere." Then I knew exactly why I had come to Laos and I was grateful to God for trusting me with this mission.

Chai said, "Doctor, you go. You are American, the war is a Lao war." But another of my helpers said, "Deep down in my heart I know that you will stick by us Lao to the end."

I, too, knew that I would stick with them. I talked

things over again with Earl and Dwight. This was a struggle for the spirit of man. We were lucky to be given a chance to help. We decided that we would never abandon these people. We would stay in Muong Sing as long as we were needed.

Then, suddenly, without warning, I was struck down by cancer and was ordered back to the United States for immediate surgery. The American Ambassador in Vientiane sent his own small plane to fly me out. He also sent word by the pilot that there was room in the plane for Earl and Dwight too. In a message to me the Ambassador said, "If you wish to leave your crew here, you must remember the immense responsibility that you fling on them."

I turned to Dwight and Earl. "This is your decision, boys," I said. "You can get on the plane and leave with me or you can remain and continue to work alone."

Without a moment's hesitation they elected to stay. "Doctor, you go on," they said. "We will stay here and take care of things until you come back."

Thank God for men like mine.

The plane revved up its motors and as it took off I looked back. There were Dwight and Earl, two young Americans, standing on the very rim of the Red hell. With them were a group of my Lao nurses and interpreters. All of them had come out to the airfield to say goodbye to me. I watched the boys below me until the mist swirled around them and I could no longer see them. The spirit that was in Earl and Dwight was the same spirit that made other young men cross the American prairies years and years ago. This is the spirit that can keep the world free for free men to live in.

Weeks passed. My operation was over and I was ready to be discharged from the hospital. They let me out a little ahead of time because I was anxious to go to the United Nations on Labor Day, 1959. This was the day that the kingdom of Laos, to which I had given so much of my time and my love, was scheduled to lay its cause before the highest tribunal on earth: the United Nations.

The Secretary General, Dag Hammarskjold, had called an emergency meeting of the Security Council. I was able to secure a seat in the press section and, still swathed in bandages, I hobbled into the United Nations building. The U.N. Security Council meets in a magnificent room. Seated before me were some of the greatest minds in the world. As I listened to them discussing the great problems of Communist conquest, the little village of Muong Sing seemed insignificant for a moment. And yet, I thought, the whole United Nations is based upon a concept of the importance of the individual. The importance of people like Chai, Si, Ngoan and my Kha Kho tribesman.

Had I been able to see into the future on that troubled Labor Day, I would have known that before the end of November, the whole Laos crisis would have passed into history. Within a few weeks of that September afternoon, the United Nations sent an observation team to Laos to investigate the war. Miraculously the war quieted down. America did a good job. Laos did an even better one. The U.N. had proved that it was able to answer a challenge.

I left the United Nations building just as the sun was

setting. The East River had a peaceful look. I hailed a cab and asked the driver to take me back to my hotel.

The driver adjusted the rear view mirror, looked back at me and said, "You been to the U.N. ain't ya, Mac?"

"Yes," I said. But my mind was far away. I closed my eyes and conjured up the village of Muong Sing. Again I saw the mountains of my beloved Laos, its great gorges and the big clouds rolling slowly up the slopes of the high rain-forest. I could see the green valleys and the huddle of dirty, thatched huts that was the village of Muong Sing. And most clearly of all I saw the sick and the old and the wretched and I knew my boys were there, taking care of them.

The place of honor for a doctor is at the bedside. Memories surged through my mind, memories of the villagers and their needs. Now that I was a full-fledged member of the fellowship of pain, now that I bore the mark on my own body, I should be able to do a better job than ever before.

Soon I would be on my way back to Laos to do the work I loved best. But first I must make some speeches, write a book, talk on radio and television, all to raise money for MEDICO. Then in December I would fly back to Laos. By Christmas I would be home again in Muong Sing, home in my hospital, home with my villagers.

"You know a lot about Communism in Southeast Asia, don't you, Mac?" the taxi driver was saying, looking at me again in his little mirror, studying my face and the way I was hunched over in the back seat. A moment later we pulled up at my hotel.

As I climbed stiffly out of the cab, I handed the driver a dollar. He looked at me and shoved the bill back into my hand. He had recognized me. "Never mind, Dr. Dooley," he said. "I'll pay your fare. You keep that buck and get back as soon as you can to your kingdom of Laos."

I felt warm and good inside. I turned and smiled at my fellow American. "O.K., Mac," I said. "Shall do."